Fit, Fifty and Fired Up

Fit, Fifty and Fired Up

One man's witty and inspiring account
of taking a risk to chase a more joyful life

Nigel Marsh

ARENA
ALLEN&UNWIN

First published in 2012

Arena Books, an imprint of
Allen & Unwin
Sydney, Melbourne, Auckland, London

83 Alexander Street
Crows Nest NSW 2065
Australia
Phone: (61 2) 8425 0100
Fax: (61 2) 9906 2218
Email: info@allenandunwin.com
Web: www.allenandunwin.com

Cataloguing-in-Publication details are available
from the National Library of Australia
www.trove.nla.gov.au

ISBN 978 1 74237 918 0

Internal design by Darian Causby
Map by Guy Holt
Set in 12.5/17.6 pt Adobe Garamond Pro by Bookhouse, Sydney
Printed and bound in Australia by Griffin Press

10 9 8 7 6 5 4 3 2 1

For my darling Mum

'Your time is limited,
so don't waste it living someone else's life.'

Steve Jobs

introduction

I'll never forget my first day at work in Australia.

To be fair it's not difficult to remember the date as it was the eleventh of September 2001, or 9/11 as the Americans call it. My wife and I had moved ourselves and our four young children to Australia from the UK four days earlier, and on the morning in question I was so busy getting ready for my job that I hadn't watched or listened to the news.

I was a bit surprised when I turned up at my office. While I hadn't been expecting a brass band or lines of bunting to greet me, I had thought I might at least be met at reception and shown to my desk. Instead, my new colleagues were huddled around TV and computer screens and no one so much as glanced at me. Understandable if you knew they were watching the twin towers collapse in lower Manhattan, but confusing behaviour if you weren't aware of what had just happened in the US.

That was ten years ago. More recently, Kate, my wife of twenty years, set off for her first day at work in Australia. She too walked into an office to find everyone huddled around TV and computer screens. Turns out news of Osama bin Laden's death was breaking.

It makes me reflect on all we've experienced as a family in between those two cataclysmic dates in modern history.

I often say that people overestimate what they can achieve in one year and underestimate what they can achieve in ten. The last decade has certainly proved that true in my life. I started out my time in Australia with a crusading new-country-new-start-new-improved-Nigel passion. I wanted to get healthy, cut down on my drinking and try to limit the excessive spillover of work into family time. Basically, to be more comfortable in my own skin, have better balance and be happier with my contribution to the world. After a year I realised that I'd still hardly scratched the surface. Yet ten years on it would be no exaggeration to say I'm an entirely different person to the one I was then. In no way perfect, but definitely different. So I'm left to wonder: what will my life be like ten years from now?

More to the point, what will *your* life be like in ten years? Take a moment to think about it. Could you be postponing joy and happiness by waiting for the right opportunity to come along – the one that finally allows you to be the real you?

I remember reading an observation by the author Jane Shilling: 'Turns out that what I did while I was waiting for my real life to begin *was* my life.' It was a lesson I took to heart. As I've got older I've become increasingly convinced not only that we shouldn't wait to see how life pans out, but that it's incumbent on us to take personal responsibility for the type of life we'd like to lead – because *not* choosing *is* a choice. To put it another way, we shouldn't leave it up to others to decide how we'll spend our one brief period of existence on this planet. Whether we like it or not, we are the people we decide to be. But how do we decide who we want to be? And when we've decided, how do we go about realising that vision? And if we do succeed in creating a life we're proud of, how do we sustain it? As Anton Chekhov noted, 'Any fool can face a crisis, it's day-to-day living that's the real challenge.'

Reflecting on the question of how I can make the second half of my life worthwhile and fulfilling has led me to pick up my pen again ten years after the events I recounted in *Fat, Forty and Fired*. As the title suggests that book describes the year I lost my job at the age of forty. It was a momentous twelve months, during which I turned the telescope around and tried to put the things that were important to me at the centre of my life as opposed to letting them languish at the edges.

Fit, Fifty and Fired Up isn't as neat as *Fat, Forty and Fired*. Life rarely is. It's not the story of a life-changing year 'off'. This time around, I'm writing about a period where I am mostly in work – of one form or another. Rather than having a perfect narrative arc, *Fit, Fifty and Fired Up* is a more messy collection of reflections from my continuing struggle to juggle work, family and life a decade later. I'm not claiming to have the answers for anyone else – or that my story is particularly dramatic. There are hundreds of books in the shops recording the achievements of remarkable people – this is not one of them. No, what follows is simply the story of how I feel as, with some uncertainty, I face my fifties.

1

Fit, Fifty and Fabulous?

I should start with a confession. When I began writing this book I was not yet fifty. Nor was I particularly fit. I was actually somewhat chubby. But the thing was, having started my fifth decade fat, forty and fired, I dreamed of ending it fit, fifty and fabulous.

Easier said than done. I could see the potential for my life to become a series of disappointments and compromises. So when a friend of mine quoted his personal trainer as saying, 'At fifty, you are the person you will be for the rest of your life', it was a very sobering thought for me. I decided that if I wanted to have some control over what my old age would be like, I needed to take action straight away – before it was too late.

So much for resolutions. Still, I might have left things to amble along if not for a visit to my father while on a trip to the UK. Dad had been living in a nursing home for the last six years. Since Dad suffered from both Parkinson's and Lewy body dementia, visiting him was not exactly a laugh riot. It'd been a couple of years since he'd been able to communicate.

Certificates from his distinguished career in the navy lined the walls of his room. I hope they provided Dad with a glimmer of recognition or pleasure in his rare moments of mental clarity; they only served to remind me of the cruel contrast between his past and present situations. But it was the pictures around the room, not the certificates, that reduced me to helpless tears. They showed Dad in happier times, when he was still vibrant, charismatic and healthy. There were pictures of him smiling and handsome, hugging my kids, at a dinner table with Mum, in his naval uniform, with my brother's family, overseas on holidays, larking around wearing a silly hat on a beach with my brother and me. Each of these photos represented a special and unique memory, and had been put there to remind Dad of how loved he was and what a wonderful life he'd lived. They were like a knife to my heart.

By late 2009 his health had grown steadily and distressingly worse. I asked Kate to keep the kids back for a while so I could visit Dad by myself first. Talking to someone who can't respond, who gives no sign that he even knows you're there, is hard enough for an adult let alone a child, so I tended to visit Dad alone or limit the time the kids spent with him.

It turned out to be a wise decision because I took one look at Dad and promptly burst into tears. Great – barely two minutes in and I was already blubbing like a baby.

Dad, Johnathon and me, Mothecombe Beach, Devon, 1966

After composing myself I spent half an hour telling Dad about the family, how everyone was fine and how much we loved him. As usual, Dad showed not a flicker of recognition.

I was so upset after we left Dad that I asked Kate to take the kids to lunch so I could go for a walk by myself. While wandering around the cold wintry streets, I couldn't help thinking that no matter how clever or special we might think we are, we're all headed for the same place. Life really is short and most definitely not a dress rehearsal. It's so easy to meander through life and only realise too late that you've wasted the chance to spend time on the important things.

As I rejoined Kate and the kids I knew something had changed in me. If it was true that at fifty you were the person you'd be for the rest of your life, I couldn't just go back home and carry on as normal. I would have to make some changes.

Spot the Difference

There was little time to act on my reflections when we got back to Australia, with the family returning almost immediately to our normal, busy – and strangely loud – routine.

As is the case for many working fathers with school-age kids (at this point Alex was fifteen, Harry was twelve and both Grace and Eve were ten), my family life often felt like one long noisy blur. At work I was used to being in control; at home it was thinly disguised chaos.

Ten years of getting our four kids to school on time, properly dressed and prepared, had sent me prematurely grey. It never ceased to amaze and irritate me that when I gave them orders, rather than simply obeying me, they debated them. (I suppose I should have recognised the warning signs that were evident from an early age. The first time I enthusiastically threw Harry a ball and said, 'Catch!', he responded, 'Why?')

And the chaos wasn't limited to weekdays. If anything, the weekends were *worse*. How this could be possible given neither Kate nor I had any work commitments on Saturday and Sunday was beyond me, but the endless round of sport, birthday parties and the like frequently brought the pressure to boiling point.

About the only oasis of calm amid the frantic activity during a typical week in our family came on Sunday evening with our regular weekly walk to the Indian takeaway to pick up dinner. This was one of my favourite times with the kids. We took the dog and just messed around and nattered as we strolled up the hill.

Next to the curry house was a video shop and a corner store, so the kids invariably ended up convincing me to rent them a movie and then buy ice cream or chocolate to round out the movie-going experience.

One of my secret guilty pleasures of these outings was to flip through the stack of gossip magazines on the counter of the curry house as we waited for our order. It didn't really matter if the magazines were a few months – or even years – out of date, because I always found reading about Brad and Jen's relationship dramas or Oprah's weight problems strangely comforting. They reminded me there are some things that just don't change in this world.

One Sunday, after a frantic day of dropping off and picking up kids, I was flicking through the stack of magazines while we waited for our takeaway when I noticed a magazine I hadn't seen before. Intrigued, I chose it over my normal reading fare of three-year-old *NW*s and *Woman's Day*s from six months before.

Cosmetic Surgery was the title of the magazine, which surprised me because I couldn't imagine a whole magazine being devoted to this one topic. Surely it was just an advertising wraparound or a dummy copy? But no, it turned out to be for real. Flicking through its two hundred or so glossy pages of articles, pictures and features on the joys of cosmetic surgery, I was struck by the fact that such a magazine could exist. What did it say about us as a society? Still, it was creepily fascinating – until, on page 43, I came across an ad that truly shocked me. Not, I hope, because I'm a prude, but because of what it said about the lengths some people will go to in order to make women feel ashamed of their bodies and therefore submit themselves, expensively, to the knife.

CORRECTIVE LABIAL SURGERY! screamed the headline, with the rest of the page largely taken up by two close-up photos of a hairy vagina. The photos were arranged side by side, the captions under them reading *Before* and *After*. Now for reasons that I'd rather not go into too deeply (let's just say a misspent youth and a past penchant for porn), I've seen my fair share of hairy vaginas, but no matter how closely I studied them the two pictures looked exactly the same to me. I couldn't spot the difference.

My careful study was interrupted by a loud and disapproving, 'Excuse me, do you mind?' from the elderly lady behind me in the queue. She was clearly disgusted to find the father of four young kids peering intently at what appeared to be pornography in her local curry shop.

'What were you looking at, Daddy?' asked Grace, my eldest daughter and, with her twin sister Eve, one of the sweetest girls on the planet.

'Nothing, sweetheart,' I replied, hastily shuffling the magazine back into the pile.

'Show us,' said Eve.

'Yeah, show us, Dad,' my younger son chimed in.

Fortunately I was saved from further embarrassment by the arrival of our food order.

On the walk home, I thought about the messed-up society we live in. Call me a bluff old traditionalist, but whatever the ads say, cosmetic surgery on your lady lips is not really likely to be the path to happiness. I feared for my daughters – and, for that matter, my sons. What on earth were my boys going to think if, in their courting years, they ever came up against a woman who *didn't* have unobtrusive labia or *hadn't* waxed herself into a landing strip or Brazilian?

If it's occasionally challenging being a man facing fifty, I mused, what the hell must it be like to be a woman, with all the extra crap they have to deal with? Only the week before I'd been buying a bottle of water from a café when I noticed five middle-aged women who looked like they'd had a group discount from the same plastic surgeon. They all sported trout pouts, shiny foreheads and exaggeratedly arched eyebrows, with not a facial wrinkle in sight. Yet none of them (from the evidence of their hands and necks) could have been a day under fifty. While they looked grotesque to me, I could only imagine the pressure any of them might feel if she were the only one in the group who chose *not* to have surgery and to look her real age.

The American phrase 'the new normal' sums up what's happening here. A good friend of mine who works in the media swears that there is not a single female TV newsreader over thirty who doesn't have Botox injections as a matter of routine. It's getting to the stage where it's normal to look like a plastic doll and shameful to mature naturally.

My encounter with *Cosmetic Surgery* didn't just make me think about unhealthy female body issues and our increasing inability to cope with ageing gracefully, it also brought me back to the thoughts I'd been having about my work and life. I had worked in the advertising industry for over twenty years and although I had issues with some of the things I'd witnessed, I'm in no way one of those 'advertising is evil' people – I'm proud of the work I've done, in fact. I've spent many wonderful years in advertising and met some truly fabulous people. Indeed, I even married one. But I was increasingly questioning the point of my labours. It wasn't so much that there was anything wrong with the advertising industry, it was more that there wasn't enough right with it. While I'd never worked on a corrective-labial-surgery account, I still couldn't help feeling that the advertising world's contribution to the overall happiness of society was, shall we say, minimal. The whole point of advertising is to get people to buy more stuff or 'improve' themselves and, to be honest, I wasn't convinced that either was really the answer to the world's ills. I wanted to be engaged in labour that had more heart.

I spoke to Kate about my misgivings, and she agreed that if this was the type of pretentious self-indulgent musing that a simple trip to the curry house brought on, maybe a change to regain some perspective might be a good idea.

3

Six Fish

Another large part of my increasing desire to yet again step off the corporate wheel was my frustration at how much time a serious corporate job takes away from your family life. I know it sounds like a cliché to say, 'I'm leaving work to spend more time with my family' but that's really what I was thinking of doing. Being a senior professional in a large company made it very hard to be meaningfully engaged in the lives of my four young kids on a day-to-day basis. Whatever the spin about flexitime or child-friendly work cultures, the brutal reality of the corporate ladder means you miss huge chunks of your children's lives and, at best, fit some rushed family moments around work rather than the other way around.

Both seeing my father in the nursing home and travelling with the family around England had made spending the precious time I had left with the kids while they were still at home – and were still (reasonably) happy to be seen with me – even more important. Yet, despite valiant efforts, I'd found it almost impossible to fit this time into our normal everyday routine. As a result I was forever planning activities we could do together on weekends, signing the family up for fun runs and ocean swims – not for the events themselves, but for the sheer pleasure of spending a few hours as a family unit. Sometimes, however, I ended up booking the poor kids for things they had no interest in doing; what I thought of as special family time, they thought was a total pain in the arse. I'd also learnt that, most times, the special moments just happen rather than being organised to order. But to have those moments I needed to be with them, not at the office pretending that texted updates on the school play or sports day were a meaningful substitute.

Spending time with Kate and the kids was one of the reasons I'd come to love long car journeys. Many people I know would rather saw their legs off than spend a four-hour journey in the car with their kids, what with the bickering, the vomiting and the endless chorus of 'Are we there yet?' I understand why people install all manner of gadgets in their cars to shut the kids up. A DVD player with individual headphones can make a long trip almost pleasant. But I like the idea of us all being trapped in a metal box for a few hours and forced to engage with each other, warts and all.

During the UK trip this lesson was brought home to me in dramatic fashion when, after visiting Mum and experiencing the trauma of seeing my father in such a bad way, it was time to head north to see Kate's parents. Barely a two-hour drive in normal circumstances, this trip turned out to be anything but normal. Unbeknownst to us, we were setting off into what would turn out to be the worst snowfall in England since 1961.

Half an hour into our trip we found ourselves stuck in a twelve-mile-long queue of idling cars as a blizzard raged around us. It wasn't long before the people in the cars in front of and behind us started abandoning their vehicles and walking to shelter. On the news the next day we were to learn that more than *two thousand* cars were abandoned overnight outside Reading alone. And where were we going? Yep – Reading.

Due to budgetary constraints our hire car was – how shall I put it? – not top of the range. In fact it was the cheapest car I could legally hire, so it was not four-wheel drive and there were no snow chains in the boot. We had, at least, borrowed Kate's father's sat nav, so we did have a helpful female voice repeatedly asking us to turn into roads that were blocked off by the police or simply impassable. The sat-nav lady became such a feature of the journey that I suggested to the kids we name her.

'What about calling her Dixie?' my younger son Harry offered.

'Dixie?' I asked.

'Yeah – Dixie Normous,' he elaborated.

Cue an explosion of hilarity from his brother and sisters. And I'm sure I caught Kate smiling out of the corner of my eye.

The kids were excited by the heavy snow so the practicalities of how we were going to get to Kate's parents' house, or where we were going to spend the night if we couldn't, hadn't yet registered with them.

At one stage, after we'd inched along about five centimetres in ten minutes, we saw a huge snowman by the road.

'Hey, kids, look at the snowman,' I said.

'It's great – what shall we call him?' said Grace.

'Phil,' Harry replied.

'Phil?' I asked.

'Phil McGroin,' he answered.

What *were* they teaching him at school? I wondered as the twins collapsed into giggles.

It was at this stage that the electronic display started flashing a warning that the left rear door was open.

'Alex, mate, push your door closed for me, will you?' I asked my son.

Alex pushed the sliding door as hard as he could. The open-door light stayed on, but was now joined by an irritating electronic *bing, bing, bing* noise.

'Mate, it's still not closed,' I said.

'Yes it is. It's closed.'

We were gridlocked anyway so I got out and opened and closed it myself, to no avail. The warning light stayed on and the *bing, bing, bing* noise kept bing binging.

Amid the double-entendring and 'binging' I was actually becoming quite worried at the conditions outside. The kids, on the other hand, were having a wild time.

'Spotto!' yelled Eve, on glimpsing a yellow car.

'Spotto! Spotto!' yelled Grace. 'I saw it first.'

For some reason, they found calling 'Spotto!' whenever they saw a yellow car or van highly amusing – even more so after Harry amended the rules and started yelling 'Snotto' whenever he saw a green car.

For the next *nine hours* we crept along accompanied by an incessant *bing, bing* soundtrack and regular calls of 'Spotto!' Meanwhile, I caught up on the latest phrases they were using, something that always fascinated me. Barely three hours in and I'd already been told to 'Calm your farm' by Harry when my frustration with the weather got the better of me. 'Yeah, Dad, buy a ticket to Chilladelphia,' Eve chipped in. When Kate came to my defence she was advised to 'chillax'.

Eventually we approached Reading, only to be stopped by the police at the top of a hill on the outskirts of the city. By this time it was late at night and the snow hadn't let up at all. Ahead of us was a steep descent followed by a long, winding incline. The police were only letting one car attempt the hill at a time because so few cars were making it. The verges on either side of the road were littered with what looked like hundreds of cars.

When we were about ten cars or so from the front of the queue, we got out and watched a car set off. Down the hill it sped, then up the other side it went before going into a skid and veering straight into the hedge at the side of the road. The driver got out and trudged back down the hill on foot. The next car to set off went into the ditch on the other side of the road. Yet another stayed out of the hedge, but got caught in a wheel spin halfway up the hill and could make it no further.

It was followed by a huge Jeep/tractor affair that made it over the hill with ease, to the cheers of both the police and the waiting motorists.

Four more cars attempted the incline without success and I was starting to feel strangely like I was in one of those Japanese game shows where the guests line up one by one to attempt a pointless and ultimately painful stunt.

We got back into the car to wait our turn, and a few minutes later a policeman tapped on my window.

'Good evening, Officer,' I said, winding down the window.

'I'll say,' he replied. 'It's been quite a night. Most people are hunkering down to sleep in their cars or legging it if they live nearby. Are you sure you want to try this?'

'We've been going for nine hours so I don't think I can face giving up now,' I replied. 'What chances do you give us?'

'Well, if you've got four-wheel drive I'd say it's fifty per cent. If not, you're totally screwed,' he answered.

On hearing this, Grace started crying. The police officer, who hadn't noticed the kids in the back, apologised sheepishly for both his language and scaring the life out of them.

'What *is* that noise?' he added.

'Oh, it's the electrics. They're convinced the side door is open, though it's definitely not. It's been doing that for hours. You get used to it after a while.'

He looked unconvinced, but didn't question me futher. As he prepared to move off, he offered me the following advice: 'Stay in a low gear, don't over-rev, steer into the skid if you feel the car sliding and don't go too slowly on the way down the hill – a bit of speed actually helps.'

I thanked him, wound up the window and took a deep breath, feeling like I'd unwittingly found myself in the queue for the ski jump at the Winter Olympics.

'Is this car four-wheel drive, Daddy?' Eve asked.

'Yes,' I lied.

The boys were excited. 'Go for it, Dad!' they yelled as the policeman motioned us forward. Screw a low gear – I didn't *have* any gears. I just took the policeman at his word and hurtled down the hill.

Miraculously, we made it up the other side with barely a wheel spin. Admittedly there was one hairy skid at the bend on the brow of the hill, but by steering into it we were fine. By the time we got to the top of the next hill the whole family was hollering and hooting as if we were on a rollercoaster.

'That was fantastic, Dad!' Alex yelled.

Even Grace had stopped crying and started laughing.

'Well done, darling,' said Kate, putting her hand on my thigh.

I felt ridiculously proud. Of myself – and of the hire car. Maybe Kias weren't so shite after all.

The celebrations were interrupted by a huge fart.

'Safe!' yelled Harry.

'No! Six fish!' yelled Grace and Eve in unison, then they began punching him in the arm. This was another car 'game'. If you let one off you got punched in the arm until you'd shouted out six types of fish. Don't ask me why, I haven't a clue.

'Salmon . . . Ow! . . . Cod . . . Ow . . . Too hard, Grace,' said Harry. 'Shark . . . Trout . . . You're hurting . . . Skate . . . Octopus.'

'An octopus isn't a fish!'

'Shark,' Harry shouted.

'You've already said shark,' Eve crowed, continuing the punching.

'Groper,' Harry gasped.

The punching stopped. The smell lingered. The binging continued.

After two more hours of crawling through the snow we finally turned into Kate's parents' street. As if to prove everything had gone too well, as soon as we sighted the house the car slid into a nearby verge and, after much revving and swearing, we realised we were stuck. It was now two o'clock in the morning, pitch black and still snowing heavily, yet everyone got out, laughing and shouting, and pushed the car the last few metres home – after a journey that had taken eleven and a half hours door to door with two adults, four kids, no food, no DVDs and an awful lot of binging.

Next day, the storm was all over the morning news. CNN even led with a story hamming up the Dunkirk spirit angle. The abandoned cars, the traffic jams, the nights spent in pubs and offices, the never-ending delays, the satellite pictures of England all white, strangers helping strangers.

Soon the phone started ringing off the hook with concerned friends and family.

'Must have been awful,' was the reaction when we recounted our story.

True, it had been mildly dangerous and we were lucky to make it, but it hadn't been awful at all. In fact it was one of the best parts of the entire holiday. Fabulous, joyous and memorable. On 21 December 2009, I spent over eleven hours trapped in a car with my wife and kids – and I loved every single minute of it. I couldn't remember the last time I'd spent that amount of time with my wife and kids without electronic entertainment (well, other than Dixie Normous). By my reckoning that's at least five mealtimes in one go.

I'm not saying I wanted to leave work to sit in traffic jams in blizzards, but I *did* want to organise my life in such a way that there didn't have to be freakish circumstances for us to spend fun, quality time together.

4

Me and Steve Martin

One big question remained: if I was really serious about leaving traditional office work again, what would I do instead? Time with the kids was one thing, but for half the day they would all be at school.

I knew all too well the dangers of sitting at home with not enough to do. It's easy to become soft and directionless without a specific focus – a 'park bencher' as one of my friends calls it. You can even find yourself reading junk mail and writing to-do lists comprising things like 'Clean teeth' and 'Pants before shoes'. I remembered an occasion during a previous hiatus from work when I'd only had one thing to do that day – buy pork chops for dinner. As I ran up the hill in my pyjamas at 5 pm, trying to get to the butcher before it closed, I was thinking, 'I haven't got the time for all these jobs! I mean I've got to clean my teeth and then there's the pork chops.'

More to the point, if I was going to leave the full-time workforce, what were we going to live on? Two previous breaks from the corporate world had put paid to any notion of savings, so our financial situation was what my financial adviser had rather quaintly called 'sub-optimal'. 'Rooted', more like. There was, however, a glimmer of light on the horizon, as for the last couple of years Kate had been seriously considering going back to work. I was actively encouraging her. Not because I wanted her to return to the workforce to fund time out of it for me, but because I had always felt secretly guilty that she'd had to give up her career. It may have made perfect sense after we had kids for us to split the domestic burden along traditional lines – me bringing in the money, her bringing up the babies – but that didn't change the fact that it was a huge sacrifice for her. She had been excellent at her job and was clearly destined for the top. Although she never complained, I knew how deeply she felt it when other women told her tales of their progress up the career ladder. I believed her when she said she didn't regret her decision for a moment but, nevertheless, ten years on it seemed the time was right for her to re-enter the world of conventional work.

But wanting to do it is one thing, doing it is another. A decade away from the workforce can do terrible things to your confidence. For many women it can be a battle to maintain their self-belief and self-esteem during a lengthy child-rearing break, especially when they are frequently referred to and treated as 'merely a mother'.

On top of the personal challenges for women returning to the workforce, there is the reality of actually getting a job after a ten-year break. It's only natural for prospective employers to wonder if you've lost your edge, energy and relevance after such a long time out of the loop. Why should they take a risk on a 're-entrant' when they could simply hire someone who's currently in a job and has an unbroken career history? A friend of mine recently told me at the school gates that she'd spent seven years gaining her qualifications and twenty years building her career. Yet after a break to see her kids through to kindergarten age, she'd found it hard to get a job that paid half decently. 'I just want to earn more than I pay my babysitter,' she told me, with grim determination in her voice.

And, finally, the global economy was experiencing a pretty spectacular meltdown just as Kate was thinking about finding a job – companies were downsizing, not expanding.

So all in all, while I was hopeful about Kate's future employment, it would have been moronic to bank on it happening soon enough and successfully enough to support the family.

It was clear I needed a plan. My initial thoughts on the matter had all the hallmarks of one of Baldrick's cunning plans in an episode of *Blackadder*. Namely, that I would sing for our collective supper by writing another book.

Now it is well known that writing is about as effective as a chocolate teapot when it comes to providing a living wage. Especially in Australia. Even a bestseller pays you four-fifths of fuck-all. On top of that, my track record was patchy to say the least. I have the dubious distinction of having come up with literally the worst book title in publishing history. Might as well be famous for something, I suppose. Yes, for reasons best known to myself, and against good advice, I called my last book *Observations of a Very Short Man*.

Now, I love that title, which relates to a story about my gorgeous younger son, Harry. At the time it also struck me as self-deprecating, which was vitally important to me because I have a terror of being seen as one of those know-it-all self-help authors who think they have all the answers. None of which changes the fact that as a title it was rubbish. Understandably, given the title, many potential readers thought it was a book about short people or that I was in fact very short. Browsers in bookshops either had no interest in a height-challenged view of the world and walked on, or were fascinated by the idea and then mightily pissed off when they got home and found out that the book had nothing whatsoever to do with being short. To put it bluntly, it was nothing short of a disaster. So much so that the publishers asked me to come up with another title when it went into a second format. After much musing, and in the spirit of *Fat, Forty and Fired*, I suggested *Overworked and Underlaid*. Everyone was happy and the book was retitled.

Two weeks after *Overworked and Underlaid* went into shops, I was walking through the centre of Melbourne when I passed a huge bookshop with an impressive display of recommended new releases in the front window. And blow me down if *Overworked and Underlaid* wasn't slap-bang in the centre of the display. Even better, it was right next to Steve Martin's brand-new autobiography *Born Standing Up*. Now, I love

Steve Martin's films, his stand-up, his music – and his writing. He is a Hollywood star, hugely talented and a much-loved household name – and here I was being given equal billing with the great man.

With shameful vanity I got out my iPhone and took a picture of this testimony to my greatness before calling Kate to brag.

'Sweetheart, you'll never guess what. I'm standing on the street outside the big Borders in Melbourne and *Overworked and Underlaid* is in the front window – right next to Steve Martin's latest book. I mean, mine's prominently displayed *side by side with Steve Martin!*'

'M-A-R,' Kate replied.

'Pardon?' I said.

'M-A-R,' she repeated.

'What do you mean, "M-A-R"? What are you on about? I'm trying to tell you my boat's come in – your husband is so famous he's getting equal billing with Hollywood stars like Steve Martin.'

'They're in alphabetical order, Nigel,' she explained in a rather withering tone.

I looked again at the display and bugger me if she wasn't right. There I was, above all the Ns and beneath all the Ls, among all the Ms.

Doesn't mean I haven't kept the photo on my iPhone anyway (or that I haven't cropped it to cut out all the other books so on the 'rare' occasion I show it to someone they can't make the same deduction that my sweet wife made . . .)

Leaving aside dud titles and all the other problems of writing, there is now a whole new set of challenges that mean the possibility of making money out of writing is even more remote. I'm talking technology, more specifically e-readers like the Kindle – or the Instrument of the Devil, as I like to call it.

Last Christmas I was given a Kindle. It was a thoughtful and generous gift, but the trouble is I *love* books. Not just *reading* books but holding books, giving books, making notes in books, recommending books, scanning bookshelves and loitering in libraries and second-hand bookshops. Browsing in a bookshop is one of my favourite activities. And I not only love paperbacks, but the paper itself. And the ink. And the binding. And the glue. The whole book thing just works for me.

And then along comes the bloody Kindle – a piece of plastic crap with type on the screen. Quite apart from the horror of the useless non-book experience of reading a book from a screen on what feels like an oversized phone, it's the economic ramifications that are terrifying for writers. It's hard enough to make any money when you know the rules, but now, with e-books, Amazon, books on your mobile, Google scanning, iPads and illegal downloads, no one really knows how it's all going to end up – apart from the sure-fire guarantee that somehow writers will be paid less for their output.

At first I refused even to take the Kindle out of its box. Then, after eight days of ignoring it, politeness towards the person who'd given it to me propelled me to at least charge it up. After I did so a remarkable thing happened. To test the bloody thing out I attempted to buy an obscure book by an

American stand-up comedian. Ping! It appeared within seconds. I then thought I'd prove my point by reading a few pages to show how crap an experience it was.

And you know what? It was brilliant. Really wonderful. The iPad even better. I suspect that in years to come, packing a physical book in a suitcase to take on holiday will be like wanting to send a message by carrier pigeon rather than via email. Sort of: 'No, no I won't take that thin light Kindle with two thousand books in it. I'd rather actual books, which will be heavier, more expensive and less convenient.'

Talk about timing. I had resolved to leave my job and write a book at precisely the time books were going out of fashion. I could just about get my head around earning no money and writing for the love of it, but it's the fact that it's difficult to be next to Steve Martin on the bookshelf if there *isn't* a bookshelf, or indeed a bookshop, that I was having trouble coming to terms with.

5

The Hamster Wheel

My debate about whether to step off the hamster wheel yet again was not in any way about being anti-business. On the contrary, I believe business and the free market have an enormously important role to play in society – and, indeed, have been two of the key drivers behind much of humanity's progress. Without the desire and capacity to turn a buck we'd be a damn sight worse off. And while I take issue with many of the things Margaret Thatcher did, I do agree with her on one issue: 'The problem with socialism is that eventually you run out of other people's money.' It really is indisputable that, down the ages, the lot of humanity has been improved far more by international commerce than it has by international communism.

I also don't think that a life spent in commerce is a waste of time or in some way not worthy. People all over the world lead varied, fulfilling and useful lives labouring for companies of all shapes and sizes. They connect to their fellow workers and provide for their families via the company coin. And the inescapable fact is that the vast majority of us have to work for the vast majority of our lives. And that's fine. People in less fortunate countries would give their right arm for the types of jobs many of us complain about having to do in the so-called first world.

And yet . . . and yet . . . there's another side to the story: business life can be dull to the point of nausea – especially if you aren't the bloke who comes to work in the company helicopter. And though for many being a cog in the machine is not a problem, for others it can be a living hell. Sometimes your job can feel like a prison sentence of soul-flattening boredom in which you're condemned to sit in a cube farm and complete a never-ending list of tasks that aren't sufficiently challenging to be interesting nor sufficiently important that anyone really cares about them or takes any notice of you doing them.

To top it off, your labours may not be connected to anything *you* care about – yet you carry on working hard, year in year out, to make people you'll never meet slightly richer, all the while putting up with ridiculous mission statements and corporate speak about 'enhancing shareholder value'. This may be tolerable when you're starting out in your career, but by the time you're forty it can get to the stage where every day you come to the office, a little bit of your soul dies. And after a while, chasing 'double-digit growth' can lose its motivating power if you're not really benefiting much from said growth.

It's even more difficult if you can't really see your firm's benefit to society. I mean, let's be honest with each other – what does it *really* matter if people buy your brand of car or perfume instead of another brand?

And the sad reality is that even if you realise you aren't fulfilled in your job (like eighty-eight per cent of people sampled in a recent survey), it's so easy to be sucked in and somehow end up spending your adult life doing it anyway. It's a bit like changing your bank. You may hate the bastards with a passion, but you keep your business with them anyway. Unlike a bank, however, your job, especially if it's unsatisfying, can come to dominate the rest of your life – because demotivating, pointless work is enervating. Moreover, it's difficult to compartmentalise and have a wild, passionate, varied life out of the office if for eight hours a day your spirit feels quashed. It's nigh on impossible to be half a person at work and a full person outside.

All too often, after a few years of working in an unfulfilling job you start justifying your actions with increasingly dubious logic. For example, a friend of mine is a currency trader. Whenever we meet, he never fails to tell me how much he loathes his career.

'Fuck I hate it, Nigel,' he said last time we met.

'Still bad, eh?' I replied.

'If anything, it's getting worse,' he answered morosely.

'Any plans?' I asked.

'Yeah, I've worked out that if I can keep on for another nine years I'll be able to retire,' he said.

Nine years! I thought. There's a sort of collective societal insanity where it's reasonable to say that you're going to do something you hate for nine years because it pays the bills.

I know as much as anyone the terror of leaving regular paid employment and the gnawing fear in the pit of your stomach when you think about how on earth you're going to provide for your loved ones. But *nine years*. Surely there had to be a better way. I didn't want to be a sad and beaten fifty-year-old. I wanted to be proud of how I spent my fifties. Not in terms of how much money I made or how impressive the title on my business card was, but proud of the type of life I'd lived, the human connections I'd established and the meaningful contribution I'd made. The trouble was, it just seemed so damn difficult to step straight out of a conventional office career again. Maybe I had to leap for the net to appear, or, at the risk of sounding like I'd swallowed a self-help book, lose sight of the shore to ever go sailing anywhere worthwhile.

If business in general can be life-crushingly dull, specific businesses can take dullness to a whole new level. After twenty-five years in a service industry I'd seen all types of companies – big, small, successful, failing, international, local, privately owned and publicly quoted. I'd been privileged to work in and with many wonderful firms, but I'd also encountered more than my fair share of toxic workplaces that brought out the worst in people, with leaders who managed by fear or set their employees up to fail and made them feel bad when they did. I'd come across companies where suggesting telling the truth for a change was met with slack-jawed amazement. I've regularly seen racism, sexism, bullying, staggering selfishness, barely believable stupidity and rampant dishonesty throughout my business career. More than that, I've seen cultures where this type of behaviour is not just present, it's accepted and even encouraged. My observations of a number of companies had led me to conclude that the two most important characteristics for advancement within them were the ability to confidently spout mindless drivel and an unquestioning readiness to do as you're told by idiots.

I'll never forget the briefing I received from my predecessor on my first day in a new role.

'Nigel, there's only one thing you need to know about this firm,' he began.

'What's that?' I enquired eagerly.

'That the people in head office can be divided into two camps. There's the Cunts and then there's the Twats.'

'Err . . . what's the difference?' I asked.

'Easy. The Cunts are really clever, but they're still Cunts. And the Twats are thick as pig shit, but they're still Twats.'

Like attracts like and you can end up with the most revolting and deluded of cultures. Leadership matters, and if the head executive of an organisation has an absence of decent values and no desire to genuinely contribute to society, it inevitably sets the tone. A fish rots from the head down and all that.

Then there's the unfortunate dilemma that the higher you climb up the greasy pole, the more challenging the roles become. Not necessarily more intellectually challenging – more morally challenging. At a certain level, especially if you're in the midst of a global financial crisis, being good at your job basically means being adept at stripping costs out of an organisation. Stripping costs in many industries actually just means 'firing people'. And let me tell you, a congratulatory email from head office thanking you for 'exiting staff speedily' is not the type of affirmation I want. That said, in certain situations firing people is necessary for a firm to survive and ensure that the remaining people keep their jobs. Still, though it might be necessary, I don't have to like it. Nor do I want to become *effortlessly* good at it.

So all in all, while I was completely aware of the necessity of commerce and saw many wonderful things about business, I was also painfully aware of the less-than-wonderful things about it on a personal level. In that context, as well as my desire to play a larger role in my kids' lives, I was seriously planning another year or so out of the workforce to take stock again, to reassess my priorities so I could be happy, fulfilled and constructive in my fifties rather than miserable and full of regret.

During all this reflection I saw a fabulous video of a TED conference. These are wonderful not-for-profit events where a collection of presenters give talks (unpaid) on 'ideas they feel are worth spreading'. That's it. Such a simple straightforward brief can make for fabulously engaging and thought-provoking listening and I thoroughly recommend you check out their website. In the video, the highly successful graphic designer Stefan Sagmeister observed that the average life plan involves twenty-five years of education, followed by forty years of work, followed by fifteen years of retirement. He contended that it was perfectly acceptable, sensible even, to take five years from your retirement and spread them out one by one throughout your working life. A sort of series of gap years for grown-ups. Rather than wait to have a couple of great years off at seventy-seven and seventy-eight, he reasoned, why not bring them forward to, say, forty-seven and fifty-one? Chances are you'd enjoy and value them a damn sight more. Not only did he think it would make for happier people, more successful marriages and better parents, he argued it would make for more effective executives as energised, stimulated people tend to be better at what they do.

There's an obvious flaw in his theory, of course. It might be fine for a handsome, talented New York-based designer to keep on leaving his job and getting another one, but for many people it's not so easy. Likewise, most people can't live without an income for a year.

For me there was the additional problem that in the advertising industry there simply aren't that many senior executive positions available. People at the top of the industry understandably want to hang on to their jobs. There was every chance that if I left my job again I wouldn't be able to get another one. So attractive as the idea was, taking another career break would involve considerable – or 'mind-bendingly ludicrous and unnecessary', in Kate's words – risks.

Having taken time off from my career previously, at least I knew to expect a big drop in status if I did decide to take another break. This can be a brutal shock if you're unprepared, because the moment you leave a senior executive position you cease to count in some social groups. Immediately. You simply fall off the edge of the cliff into total irrelevance. Many people who had regarded you with admiration and treated you with respect act like you no longer exist. Telling them that you're staying at home for a year to spend more time with the family and write a book is akin to putting on Harry Potter's invisibility cloak.

I've had people literally turn around and wander off to find someone more appropriate to brag to about their ski chalet and renovations than the loser househusband-cum-writer. I'm not complaining. I don't want to position myself on any ladder, which is one of the reasons I don't mind stepping off it. I find the attitude of people who are always wanting to be seen to be progressing ever upwards deeply depressing. I'd rather spend more time working on being happy with what I've got than obsessing about how to get what I don't yet have. Kate accuses me of perversely indulging in 'one downmanship' and on this point she's right. All the dick-measuring contests are such a turnoff that on occasion I just want to prove a point, so I overcompensate in the opposite direction.

If the drop in status was not an issue for me, meaningful pursuit most definitely was. I didn't want to take time off from my career to watch more TV or have long lie-ins. I wanted to do it so I could achieve things that were well-nigh impossible while stuck on the hamster wheel.

I think goals are incredibly important because they help you turn what might otherwise be a crisis into an opportunity.

Setting goals helps you to stop dwelling on former glories. There's a huge danger if you decide to change course that you'll fail to change your criteria for success at the same time, thereby condemning yourself to feeling like a failure. Your criteria of success has to be realigned to your new goals. If you've left a senior job to spend more time with your kids, comparing your earnings to the previous year's will only ever lead to pain. Comparing how much time you're spending with your kids compared with the previous year is a much more sensible approach.

It is also important that your goals aren't all about giving things up (I'm a big one for giving things up: alcohol, smoking, shampoo, caffeine, chocolate – the last two with only partial success . . .) Some goals should definitely be about adding things *in*. For example, during my fat, forty and fired year I got enormous satisfaction out of teaching myself to swim. So as I leant ever further towards deciding to take another break I started making my usual long list of things I wanted to achieve. This time, though, I wanted to make sure any list of goals had at least a couple of items that were less solitary and self-focused. Things that I felt would genuinely benefit Kate and the kids.

When I asked Kate how I might make myself more useful to her if I resigned from my job her reply was succinct: 'Learning to stop throwing away well-paid jobs would be a good start.'

Not so much 'Behind every successful man there's a great woman'; more 'Behind every dropout husband there's a pissed-off wife'.

•

After wrestling with the decision for months I finally decided to commit to leaving the traditional workforce once again. Kate and I had debated it endlessly. I wanted to do the right thing for my family, not just myself. Encouragingly, my speaking engagements had increased, which gave me hope that I could at least earn some money after I left full-time work. I came to realise it wasn't just the harsh practical realities like financial uncertainty that were holding me back from taking the plunge into the unknown again – it was deeper, more subconscious stuff as well. In some warped way I believed that if I wasn't spending nine hours a day working I was somehow 'letting the side down'. A messy combination of Protestant work ethic, my upbringing and self-worth issues meant I felt an uncomfortable sense of shame at the thought of not pulling my weight in the traditional way. It was as if I didn't believe I deserved the right to be happy.

I grew up in a world where I was regularly told if I wasn't up and out by 7 am I had 'wasted the best part of the day'. It was considered frivolous to put energy into anything but traditional productive labour. When I spoke to my brother about this, far from laughing it off he said he knew exactly what I was talking about. He had left the army after twenty-seven years' service to set up his own consultancy practice. Three years on it was going fabulously well, yet he admitted to occasionally feeling guilty that he felt so happy. Similarly, I still feel uneasy about going to the cinema during the day because I was brought up to believe it was somehow slothful and wrong to do so.

It was Kate who finally got me over the line.

'You've got to shit or get off the pot, Nigel. You're clearly unhappy and want a change. It's not as if you haven't put the effort in – you've done twenty-five years' hard slog. I'm happy to back you if you're happy to back yourself. I'd just appreciate a little less moaning.'

I wrote my resignation letter that evening.

My employer was wonderfully understanding when I handed in my resignation and we quickly came to an agreement that I would keep the news confidential and stay working for a few months to ensure a smooth transition to my successor. This had the advantage of buying me some much-needed time to prepare for the coming dramatic change in our circumstances – or 'the abyss', as Kate called it. The kids' responses were less bleak – but typically varied. Showing a rather tenuous grasp of the financial implications, Eve wanted to know if I could now buy her a horse. Grace asked if we could go on more 'Daddy's trips'. This is where I take each of them off for an afternoon one-on-one with their Dad. Alex was delighted as he immediately worked out it significantly increased our chances of getting to the Rugby World Cup in New Zealand. Harry simply asked, 'Should we call you "Shirker Tensing" again, Dad?' He was referring to the name they came up with for me the last time I'd taken a break and had spent a year dodging the chores.

It was both liberating and scary to have actually resigned. While on the one hand those American self-help authors have a valid point when they say, 'Leap and a net will appear', so too did the French revolutionaries when they said, 'The impending guillotine certainly focuses your mind'. In Kate's case this meant focusing on how to keep the family afloat once my salary disappeared. In my case it inevitably involved drawing up a new list of goals . . .

6

Tin Dinner

One of the goals I decided was essential during my next hiatus was to teach myself to cook. It might seem like a sad, trivial and boring objective to you (and it certainly wouldn't make us any money), but I knew if I became a better cook it would have a huge positive impact on my family – far more than completing an ocean race or another new business presentation, fun or lucrative though those things might be.

You see, for the previous sixteen years Kate had invariably had to cook the family's dinners. Not because I'm lazy – well, not *just* because I'm lazy – but because I was utterly and completely useless in the kitchen. Having been sent to boarding school very young, I just never learnt to cook.

On one memorable occasion at college my then-girlfriend caught me late at night in the kitchen.

'What the hell are you doing?' she asked.

'Cooking us a snack,' I replied proudly.

'By pushing an unopened tin of beans around an empty saucepan?' she asked.

'Yeah. It says on the label to put it in a saucepan and heat it.'

'You've got to *open* the tin and put the beans *in* the saucepan, you idiot.' Her expression was one of utter incredulity.

In my defence I was rather drunk at the time, but you get the point – it was a very low base I was working from.

Left to my own devices I bought takeaway or made delectable delicacies like, er, toast. Consequently, when I was left to look after the kids *they* ate takeaway or toast. And if there's one thing Kate is obsessive about, it is feeding the kids properly.

Much to my horror Kate has always spent eye-watering sums on organic produce – preferably fruit and veg that has been sung to and animals that have been cuddled. All of it arrived at our house in an expensive box each week so Kate could cook us all healthy meals. The never-ending grind of preparing the family's dinners night after night really got her down sometimes, especially given her efforts were not always, shall we say, fully appreciated. The kids would happily eat nothing but pizza and curry. To this day Harry's favourite meal is 'Tin Dinner'. I could understand how galling it must be, after you'd slaved away in the kitchen chopping fresh herbs and veg, to have your twelve-year-old son come home from school begging, 'Please, Mum? Please can we have Tin Dinner?' The poor sod has eaten so much freshly prepared organic food that he thinks heavily processed tin food is a treat.

It took me a while to realise that offering to 'cook' the family meal in a way Kate hated (i.e. buying takeaway) wasn't helping. If I really wanted to do something loving and lastingly useful for Kate *I needed to do it the way she wanted it to be done*. To help me get my head around the whole topic of cooking I asked that my Christmas present be an old Jamie Oliver book called *The Ministry of Food*; it had the very promising subtitle: *Anyone can learn to cook in 24 hours*. While in my case Jamie was wildly overreaching himself, I liked the general principle of the book, which was designed for culinary idiots who can't boil an egg and don't know what coriander is.

Kate was pleased but highly sceptical when I shared my idea about learning to cook.

'You'll cook healthily for the kids and me?'

'Yep, for the whole family,' I answered.

'Will you leave the kitchen a mess and expect me to tidy up afterwards?'

'No I intend to plan it, buy it, cook it, serve it and wash up afterwards. You won't have to do or think about a thing,' I said with a lot more confidence than I felt.

'No takeaways or toast? Fresh healthy stuff?'

Christ, some people are hard to do a favour for, I thought.

'Only if you stop asking me questions and say thank you,' I replied stiffly.

'Oh, right . . . that *would* be great,' she said. 'When do you start?'

Not long after that I found myself in the kitchen surveying what was soon going to be my new domain. At work I was lucky enough to have a large office with all the executive accessories – sofas, fridge, gorgeous view and, importantly, a lockable door. The situation at home could hardly have been more different. For a start, our kitchen doesn't *have* a door, let alone a lock. It's just a sort of annexe that's separated from the living room by a counter. The living room itself is as far away from a private space as you can get, being an open-plan room in the centre of the house where everything happens. As well as the front door opening directly into it, the living room is the point from which you access anywhere else in the house, be it garden, toilet or bedroom. But it's not just the lack of privacy and constant foot traffic that can be problematic if you want a bit of peace and quiet – it's the sheer amount and variety of stuff that is packed into the room.

As the only communal space in the house, the living room is where the dining table is. But that's just the start. It's also where the dog sleeps in her basket and the kids do their homework. It's where the home phone is kept. And the stereo. And the family computer. And the twins' musical instruments. And my guitar. And a threadbare sofa. Nothing unusual for a large family, I suppose, but after school the place descends into barely controlled, noisy, crowded chaos.

On any given day in our living room someone will be on the phone to his girlfriend, another at the computer checking out Facebook, one learning to tap dance on our once pristine floorboards, another standing by the table practising the saxophone. Amid all this commotion Kate will invariably be fielding a call on her mobile while preparing our latest organic feast. Most days one or other of the twins will have a friend over, which would be lovely if their method of communication involved more talking and less screeching. I actually find the pitch of a nine-year-old girl's screech *physically* painful – it goes right through me in the same way as the sound of nails being dragged down a blackboard.

All it takes is for the doorbell to go and brutish hell *really* breaks loose. Our dog Mattie goes berserk. I yell for someone to shut the effing dog up and get the door. One of the twins starts crying at my rudeness. Kate yells for everyone to be quiet because she can't hear the phone. The poor visitor has to shout to be heard, often with variations of 'Is it a bad time? I can come back later.'

Should it be teatime the guest may have to witness my kids eating their tea with the table manners of badly behaved farmyard animals. It's actually beyond parody. And deeply shocking for young couples who haven't had kids yet. In fact, I've come to think of our living room as a sort of alternative contraceptive device. Many couples thinking of starting a family end up putting their plans back by at least a year after visiting us at teatime.

So, anyway, as I stood in the kitchen surveying the feral cross between a kindy and a zoo that was to become my new 'office', the hamster wheel almost seemed attractive.

I'd been thinking about this meal all week. Why wait until I actually left work to start? Why not give it a go right away? I'd gone through Jamie's book at length searching for a dish that was blindingly easy to make – and vegetarian. Yes, meat used to be the staple of our family diet but after Harry helpfully told Eve that some people ate horses she gave up all meat on the spot out of solidarity with her equine friends. As a result I needed to produce a dish that would satisfy the ethical considerations of my nine-year-old while also pleasing the palates of five ravenous carnivores. After much study I decided I'd cook Tagliatelle alla Genovese – or 'pesto pasta', as Kate rather less impressively called it.

Determined to do things *exactly* how Jamie had described in the book, I went shopping for the ingredients, which was an education in itself. It's one thing to buy '1 medium potato', but when I got to the chuffing shop I was faced with stacks of different varieties of the bloody things. Feeling like one of those dodgy sexual predators who pick up women in supermarkets, I asked a woman which type of potato to buy. Then, embarrassingly, I had to go back and disturb her again when I realised I didn't have a clue what basil *was*, let alone where it would be kept. In the end I couldn't face it anymore and asked the store owner if she'd come round with me and my list. She was remarkably helpful and in barely ten minutes I had everything I needed in my basket.

Jamie claims it takes 'minutes' to prepare this 'simple' dish, and although I'm sure that's right for him this was my first-ever attempt at making a proper family meal and it took me over an hour before I had everything ready and was prepared to drop the pasta into the boiling water.

But the thing is, I enjoyed every moment of the preparation, cooking and even serving of that meal. I realise it's easier to be excited about something you've never accomplished before than something you've done ad nauseum for sixteen years, but I loved it. As did the kids. To watch them all hoe into the food without complaint (despite the lack of meat and profusion of vegetables) was incredibly satisfying. They all had seconds. And Kate did too.

My meal wasn't a total triumph, though, since I blotted my copybook somewhat with dessert. I've always been what my brother calls 'fruit idle'. It's not that I don't *like* fruit, it's just that I find it such a pain in the arse to prepare anything involving all that peeling and deseeding. As a result, my rather lame offering for dessert on this occasion was a bowl of yoghurt and muesli – or 'bludge pudding' as Grace perceptively called it. I was true to my word, however, and cleared up, refusing to let Kate help.

On the one hand, cooking my first proper meal at age forty-seven was a small achievement in the grand scheme of things. Some would say shamefully pathetic. Indeed, as Eve rather sniffily pointed out, 'There's a difference between "heating" and "cooking", Daddy.' But for me it was momentous. In self-help circles it's common to say you become successful the moment you take a single step towards a worthwhile goal. Whether this is true or not I don't know, but when I went to bed that night I felt happier than I had for ages.

7

Dial H for Liz

Significant though it might be, cooking is merely one part of the domestic burden. Transport is an equally pressing issue. Having four kids of school age means there always seems to be an event Kate or I have to go to for one or the other of them. The sporting demands alone are almost overwhelming. It takes military precision to meet them. And it's not just the weekends that are dominated by the kids' activities, it's weekday mornings and evenings too. Twice a week we have to drop children off at sports practice at 6.45 am in different locations. Four times a week a child will have to be picked up from some far-flung location after sport or music. Then there are the parent–teacher evenings that seem to come round at least once a week. And of course the above doesn't even take into account their increasingly busy social lives, which was leading to frequent begging for lifts to all ends of the city.

It's always good, therefore, when there's a social get-together for parents in a local pub so we don't have to go too far. Not that this means we won't be late because, God love her, Kate views a starting time for an event more as a *suggestion* than an actual time to arrive by. In our twenty-year marriage this has caused more arguments than any other topic. I don't mind Kate being late when she's going somewhere by herself, but when I'm involved and it makes me late as well I can't stand it. (I come from the military school of thought whereby if you're not five minutes early, you're late.)

I went through one particularly painful stage of attempting to get Kate to things on time using a variety of strategies. The first attempt involved getting prepared early myself and then chivvying her along well in advance. Disaster. Not only were we later than ever, but she detested me pestering her. After that I tried begging, getting angry, changing the kitchen clock – all of which proved equally useless.

Our ongoing inability to get to anything on time started to make me seriously unhappy. I spoke to a friend about it and she suggested it might be an issue of control, with Kate not wanting to feel ordered around by me. I resisted the urge to suggest she was overanalysing matters and made a decision instead. I would give up and Kate and I would no longer talk about it. I would no longer rush her and she'd be happy.

And we would be late everywhere.

As we prepared for the next parents' night out at the local pub, I waited for Kate to get ready without comment.

We were already late when Kate shouted downstairs, 'Nige, I won't be much longer. Could you call Lizzie and ask her if she wants a lift?'

'Sure – what's her number?' I yelled back.

'It's in my book,' called Kate.

Going into the kitchen, I looked under L in Kate's address book, but I couldn't find it. I turned to A – for Ambrose, Lizzie's surname. Not there either.

'Are you sure she's in the book?' I yelled.

'Absolutely,' Kate replied.

I looked under L again, then A. Nope – definitely not there.

'Sweetheart, I've looked again and she's not in the book,' I called up the stairs as calmly and reasonably as I could.

'Yes she is, you dozy pillock. I wrote her in myself.'

Muttering dark thoughts, I went back into the kitchen and checked once more. No luck this time either. Then I remembered Lizzie's maiden name was O'Hare. I flicked to O, but again came up with a blank. She simply wasn't in the book.

'Darling, she sodding well isn't in the book,' I said to Kate as she finally came down the stairs.

'Oh for Christ's sake, Nigel. I told you I wrote her in myself.' Kate snatched the address book out of my hands. 'Look, there she is,' she said triumphantly, pointing to Liz's number.

'But it's under H!' I exclaimed.

'Obviously. H for O'*Hare*,' she replied.

Kate's approach to adding names to her address book is endearingly random. I could be under N for Nigel, M for Marsh, D for Daddy or P for pillock. There is no set rationale – just whatever seems like a good idea at the time. On one memorable occasion I found our London friends Simon and Rebecca under K, despite the fact that neither Simon nor Rebecca has a middle, maiden or surname that starts with the letter. Kate said, 'But they live in *Kentish* Town.' Brilliant.

Anyway, we had to drive the short distance to the parent evening because it was bucketing with rain. In the car I was quiet. Kate broke the silence.

'Nigel, I don't want you being morose tonight,' she said.

'What do you mean?' I replied morosely.

'You know full well what I mean. You're awful at these things. You go all quiet and don't talk to anyone. It makes you seem really unfriendly. I know you're not comfortable at these occasions but you have to make an effort and show an interest. Ask people about themselves. Make conversation. Please. Do it for me.'

Despite my irritation at being late and playing Address Book Roulette, I couldn't help but admit that Kate had a point. I could be awful in social situations, especially since I'd given up drinking. I tend to go into my shell if I'm uncomfortable. So, as I dropped Kate off outside the pub door so she could make up some time and not have to walk in the rain from the car park, I resolved that I'd surprise her and really make an effort – not just for her, but for me. I was sure I'd enjoy these functions more if I threw myself into them. Kate was right – it *was* high time I developed a few more social skills and stopped being a grumpy bastard.

I drove down the hill to the beach car park full of good intentions, smiling at a mum as she pulled into the space next to mine.

'Awful night, isn't it?' I said, motioning to the rain as she got out of her car.

'Mmm,' she replied non-committally.

'My name's Nigel,' I said, extending my hand.

She shook my hand limply without offering her name in return.

Now who's the unfriendly one? I thought. But never mind, I could hardly expect us to have an immediate rapport, so I ploughed on with relentless cheeriness.

'How many have you got?' I asked.

'What?' she replied.

'Kids. How many? I've got four. Two boys and two girls. It's our second lad that's in year five.'

She looked supremely uninterested and not a little suspicious.

'Grace, Eve, Harry and Alex,' I added, as if the detail went some way to prove I wasn't lying and I did actually have four kids.

Perhaps I'm just totally out of practice, I thought as we walked up the hill together. I kept asking her questions about herself, as Kate had recommended. When she kept on stone-walling me I changed tactics and told her about myself. She was even less impressed. To be frank, it was quite a relief when we got to the doors of the pub. Surely the other class mums wouldn't all be such hard work.

'Right, here we are,' I said cheerily.

She looked at me with yet another one of those strange looks she'd been giving me all the way up the hill.

'Is that your way of asking me for a drink?' she asked, barely keeping the contempt out of her voice.

It suddenly struck me then that *she wasn't going to the parent function*. She had no idea why I'd been awkwardly trying to chat her up with bizarre details about my kids. Come to think of it, I'd possibly scared the life out of her.

Whether I'd scared her or not, what was beyond doubt was that I'd just spent ten minutes trying to befriend a complete stranger with intrusive questions and intimate stories. Dozy pillock indeed.

8

The Long Goodbye

When it comes to social occasions it would be a lie to say Kate's perfect either. There is one particular quirk she has had for the twenty-two years I've known her that, while not life-threatening to anyone else, has often weakened my own will to live. For Kate, you see, is the all-time Olympic champion of the long, drawn-out social goodbye. I didn't realise there was actually a name for her affliction until last year when, during one of her all-time classic goodbyes, I was bemoaning her behaviour to our host John who said, 'Ah yes, Nigel, in our Greek community we called it the Armenian Farewell.'

I take some solace from the fact that it is a recognisable condition and that it has been named. It makes me feel more normal. Like an alcoholic introducing himself at an AA meeting I can now state stoically, 'My name is Nigel and I live with a wife who does the Armenian Farewell.'

Because the simple fact is, Kate doesn't do short goodbyes. Ever. She never says goodbye and then actually *leaves* a social function. Oh no. Kate's first goodbye is merely the warm-up act before the serious round of goodbyes starts. And this doesn't just involve walking around and saying goodbye – at length – to everyone. It involves saying goodbye to the *same people* repeatedly. In different locations. Once she's gone round everyone she simply starts at the beginning again. It's as if I'm stuck in some particularly bleak version of hell where the torment has no end. When there is a natural break in the conversation she spurns the perfectly polite opportunity to move on and instead poses another open-ended conversation-extending question. The process rarely takes less than an hour. And I promise I'm not exaggerating. At the last dinner party we were at I made a point of quietly observing the process in detail to check I wasn't inventing the issue.

At 11.30 pm Kate said to the host, 'That was lovely! Thank you *so* much. We really must go now as our babysitter has to be home by midnight.' A long conversation then ensued about just how lovely the evening had been and how we must do it again soon, etc., etc. Everyone then got up and Kate started clearing the table and taking dishes to the kitchen. This sparked a round of 'Oh please don't, Kate. Leave it for us and we'll do it later,' and 'Oh no it won't take me a minute. I'll just do the big dishes that won't fit in the dishwasher.' We then had fifteen minutes of goodbyes in the kitchen. Moving to the sitting room while coats were retrieved for us, Kate initiated an entirely new thread of conversation that went on for so long that the male host and I actually sat down. Ironically, twenty minutes later Kate barked, 'Come on Nigel, get up, we're late, we have to go,' which was as painful as it was familiar.

But we were only barely *halfway* through the ordeal, as the goodbye/thanking process simply moved to the hall. Then we spent another ten minutes chatting on the front doorstep, before walking to the front gate and having a yarn there as well. Leaving our hosts' property didn't provide any respite either as, after we walked to where our car was parked, we proceeded to *stand next to it* talking rather than get in it. Even eventually physically getting in the car wasn't enough to bring the evening to an end. While sitting in the car Kate carried on talking through the open passenger-side window while I did my best not to rev the engine – or indeed pour petrol over myself and light a match. I swear she was still mid-goodbye as I finally drove off after receiving the second of the 'Where the hell are you?' texts from the babysitter. Eighty minutes from first goodbye to actual physical departure. Not a record but pretty impressive all the same. When I'm with the kids we go and sit in the car and place bets on when Kate will finally join us – it's taken over from 'Spotto' as the kids' favourite car game.

The process is actually worse at a proper party. The more people to say goodbye to, the longer the performance. Given that we're usually late everywhere, I've worked out that on many occasions if we're to have any hope of leaving on time we would have to ring the doorbell and immediately say, 'Hi. Lovely party. We really have to go now. Many thanks for having us,' before stepping inside. We could then walk around saying farewell to everyone in all the different required locations and be out in time for the babysitter not to sue us.

I have no idea if this is how people actually behave in Armenia, but I've irreversibly stroked the country off any future travel plans just in case.

9

Porker

Since learning to swim during my first year off, I've made a point of doing at least one rough-water ocean race a year. I love them – they're one of my all-time favourite things about living in Australia because they're invariably in stunning locations, the atmosphere is joyous and the races themselves are both challenging and invigorating. But beyond the sheer enjoyment I like to do at least one a year because they keep me honest. There's just no faking it. To my mind, if I can swim from Shelly to Manly or Bondi to Bronte, I can't have totally given up on life – irrespective of how slow I go or how awful I look in my budgie smugglers. I may get beaten by every other swimmer (in fact I *usually* get beaten by every other swimmer – which is not really surprising given my standard race plan is 'start slow then taper off'), but at least I beat all the people who don't enter. Not so much 'back of the pack', more 'front of the rest'. While I may be setting my sights too low I don't *want* to have to run a marathon or climb Everest to get a sense of achievement and self-esteem. A kilometre or so in the ocean will do for me.

Collecting your race cap before an ocean swim can be a pretty sobering experience. It involves walking past a long line of tents to get to the tent for your age group. And standing around with the cap on after you've retrieved it can be even more sobering because you can't kid yourself, or anyone else, that you're still thirty-five if you've got a bit of green plastic on your head that screams, 'I'm officially forty-four to forty-nine.'

I find the beach before the starting gun a fascinating lesson in how the human body ages; everyone is basically naked and grouped on the basis of how old they are. It's what it would be like if everyone went to the train station in just their underwear at rush hour. If you're doing an ocean race and you've got a large gut it's there for the whole world to see, not hidden under a well-cut suit or baggy shirt. It's a wonderful leveller – as well as liberating. No matter how clever or powerful you think you are, standing on a beach in your Speedos will strip you of any externally garnered status symbols.

The most noticeable thing about all the bodies on show before a race isn't so much how awful or wonderful people look with their kit off, but how different bodies can be. In my age group there are women who are in considerably better shape than those in the twenty-four to twenty-nine group. As I stood on Bondi Beach before one race I looked around at the other men my age. Of course, you had to be active enough to do an ocean swim to be there, but still, the contrast was amazing. On the one hand you had men with perfect V-shaped torsos, flat stomachs and bulging muscle definition on their arms, and on the other hand you had . . . well, people like me. Pasty and flabby.

The truth was, I had let myself go before this particular ocean race. I wasn't quite back to my fat, forty and fired weight, but I did have a large beer belly – which was particularly annoying considering I hadn't had a single beer for over eight years. Brilliant, really – all the downside of looking like Homer Simpson and none of the upside of being able to drink in Moe's tavern.

It's just so easy to put on a couple of pounds a year until before you know it you're half a stone overweight and complaining that your jeans have shrunk. As I looked around at the taut stomachs and rippling muscles that day it struck me that we all have a choice about letting ourselves go versus staying trim.

Society's standards about weight and food seem to have slipped inexorably over recent years so that it's harder than ever to make the right choices. Last time I was in America I was stunned at how fat people were. Enormous, grossly overweight people puffed around shopping malls and no one seemed surprised or shocked. What's worse is that according to a recent survey over thirty per cent of grossly overweight Americans have no intention of ever losing weight. They see nothing wrong with their size. The net effect of this is that acceptable body norms have subtly changed. Being two stone overweight with a beer gut is now considered relatively 'in shape' for a man, though in reality it's nothing of the sort – it is two stone overweight with a beer gut.

That Bondi ocean race occurred at a critical moment in my life. Approaching fifty and overweight it would have been easy to relax my standards and think: What the hell? It's only a couple of stone before slipping into an old age of irreversible fatness. Alternatively, I could say, 'Bugger that' and make an attempt to reverse the decline before it was too late. Looking around at the other competitors, I chose the latter. I didn't want to be a porker in my fifties. I wanted to attain the standards of the ocean swim starting line, not the standards of the shopping mall checkout line.

I'm not talking here about being one of those fitness freaks who Clive James wonderfully described as 'looking like a fistful of walnuts in a condom'. No, I'm talking about being the right weight for your age and height and having a flat stomach. The fact that my ambition to lose weight seemed an enormous unscaleable mountain as I stood on the beach that day, only served to demonstrate that I had let myself slip mentally. Why the hell couldn't I be trim? It was *my* life. And my choice.

Easier said than done, but hey, what's the point in taking time to reassess if you aren't going to act on the assessment?

•

Deciding to lose weight is one thing; implementing it is another. I found it hard to focus on it as a goal. It was just too easy to hide behind the competing demands of the office and the kids. Like the classic alcoholic, I was putting off addressing the real issue until 'after things had calmed down and I was a little less busy'. Yeah right, as if that was ever going to happen. But despite my busyness and failure, weight-wise, I was actually increasingly happy. The kids were all content at their schools. Kate had been offered a part-time job. Even the semi-permanent floodwater in our basement had receded. On top of all that, having resigned gave me clarity and a goal to work towards – my last day in the office. At times I found myself feeling positively euphoric and made the schoolboy error of mentioning this to Kate.

'Nigel, happiness is merely the temporary illusion that things aren't going to change for the worse,' was her sobering reply.

While I don't share Kate's pessimistic view of the world, it would be a lie to say I wasn't worried. In fact, a regular nightmare I'd been having since my late twenties returned with increasing frequency. This was the dream from which I would wake up sweating in the middle of the night, terrified that I hadn't done any revision for the major school exam I was taking in the morning. The relief I felt when I woke up and discovered I wasn't a fifteen-year-old schoolboy on the eve of an unprepared-for exam was always intensely joyous. You didn't have to be a qualified therapist to realise that, irrespective of how committed I was to the path I was on, deep down I had huge subconscious concerns about our future.

Worried or not about the future, I was still overweight in the present. And I wanted to lose weight before my last day in the office and start my new life on the front foot. With some momentum. Losing a few kilos seemed as good a way to do this as any other. I had successfully lost a lot of weight in the past so I decided to review what had worked for me then in a bid to get back on track.

Ever since the publication of *Fat, Forty and Fired*, people have written to me asking how I lost so much weight and how I'd advise them to get in shape. Although I've written back to everyone thus far, I've always resisted the urge to go into any detailed advice – relying instead on a jokey 'eat less' reply. The truth is, I believe it's not so much about what you eat as what you *think* that influences your ability to lose weight.

Hundreds of new and different diets are launched every year, but to me they all miss the point. We all know *how* to lose weight – simply eat fewer kilojoules than you expend. This has always been the answer and always will be. No, the real challenge is about finding a way to motivate yourself to do it. The battle is won or lost in the mind, not in the gym or with a fitness trainer.

There are three key pillars to my amateur weight-loss 'program' – patience, delaying gratification and honesty.

Patience is probably the most important. I don't want quick but unsustainable weight loss, I want permanent improvement. More than that – I want permanent improvement that is *easy and enjoyable to live with*. I want to reach a new weight and then stop thinking or worrying incessantly about food and weight. It's a bit like it was with my drinking. I want to sort the issue out, then move on.

As a result, I deliberately set the bar low. While some personal trainers and diet-book authors would have you losing up to two kilos a week – and *The Biggest Loser* would have you losing four kilos – I aim to lose one pound (approximately half a kilo) per week. Setting such an achievable weekly target is vital for me because it takes away any excuses I might have.

So often in life we get carried away and set goals for ourselves that in our hearts we don't really believe in. And though they may be motivational at the time we set them, in reality all they do is set us up for failure. If you say you're going to lose a stone, or five kilos, in a month and two weeks later it's clear you aren't going to make it, you can say to yourself: 'Well, I was never going to do it anyway.'

If I say I'm going to lose a pound a week, the only reason for failing will be that I haven't followed through on an easily achievable target I was serious about. If I can't lose a pound a week, it's *not* because of my metabolism, friend's wedding, how busy I am at work or lack of money. It's because I haven't taken the simple actions required to lose one single lousy pound in seven whole days. The downside of the achievable approach is that losing weight can seem like a long, slow process with frustratingly little evidence of success. This is where patience comes in. A virtue that doesn't come naturally to many of us, patience is something you need to cultivate in order to lose weight.

But being patient won't get you anywhere if you can't develop the capacity to delay gratification. You need to get used to feeling a pang of hunger and *not* immediately satiating it by putting something in your mouth. Not easy, especially in today's instant-fix world. But like patience, delaying gratification is a skill that *can* be learnt. New habits take weeks to develop – and initially you may feel some discomfort – but once you've mastered doing things differently, you can achieve amazing things.

The idea of delaying gratification puts me in mind of a cricket-mad teacher at school who told me how, when his father was in a remote part of colonial Africa, he couldn't get the papers on a daily basis. Instead, he got them delivered in three-month batches, upon which he would immediately lock them in the attic – bringing them down one day at a time in chronological order. Each day they'd read the Test match updates and go to bed eagerly awaiting news of the next day's play – even though they could easily have run up the stairs and read the results for the whole series there and then. Apparently the suspense and enjoyment was every bit as real as if they were actually following the games live.

I'm not saying you need to go to that sort of extreme, but if you're going to successfully lose weight you do have to mentally discipline yourself so that when you fancy a chocolate bar (or whatever) you don't give in there and then, but decide you'll have it later if you successfully reach that week's target weight.

Which brings me to the last of my three pillars: honesty. From the start to finish of any successful weight-loss program, you need to be prepared to be totally honest with yourself. Before I embark on a serious mission to lose weight, I ask myself whether I'm actually committed to the weight loss I've designated. Am I ready to take myself seriously and commit to achieving my goal, or is it just a fleeting hope that I'll give up on as soon as things get difficult or I feel slightly hungry?

If I can answer this question positively, then losing one pound a week ceases to be a big ask. The next step is to remain honest as I progress. To help me be so I ignore what the experts say and weigh myself *every day* at the same time, in the same place, wearing the same thing. For me, it's first thing in the morning, in the bathroom, naked. ('Ewww, Dad, get some clothes on,' Eve says whenever she walks in and is confronted by the vision of me naked on the scales.)

Each day I write down my weight and at the end of the week I take my *heaviest* weight. This is important as I don't want to fall into the trap of being one of those people who starve themselves before their weekly weighing day and stand on the scales having just been to the loo and taken all their jewellery off. I want the satisfaction of *real* weight loss.

So that's my thinking. As for the particular type of diet, there isn't one. I just honestly examine what food I've been consuming and cut back ever so slightly, choosing one thing a week to change. Maybe it's the toast with breakfast. Or the afternoon chocolate. Or the pudding at dinner. Or it may just be a matter of adjusting my portion sizes. Whatever. I pick one thing and stick with it – and I pick something *easy*. If you're out of shape and want to lose weight, you'll probably be spoilt for choice about the things you know you can change. I know I am. On a normal day my food intake consists of a big breakfast, mid-morning snack, two-course lunch, mid-afternoon snack and some nibbles before a two-course dinner. I also generally have a couple of full-fat milk drinks and a can or two of full-sugar cola throughout the day.

The secret for me isn't in going from that to baby portions of rabbit food, it's to slowly and steadily *marginally* improve my behaviour. Giving it all up in one go is too much to face, but cutting out the nibbles before dinner is hardly a big ask.

How do I know if it's working? Easy. At the end of the week if my weight hasn't gone down by a pound I'm either not being honest with myself about my real behaviour or I need to change something extra. If it's the former I admonish myself to grow up and stop wasting my time. If it's the latter, the 'Stop moaning and eat less, you fat bastard' rule applies – I examine my intake and choose one extra thing to change. I know it looks simple. It is. But I promise you it works. Or at least it did last time I tried it.

That's not to say it isn't challenging. All change is challenging. New habits take a few weeks to form. For many of us it's a new experience to actually feel hungry and not immediately eat something. But be patient and learn to delay gratification, be honest and focus on what you want in your life – not on what you're denying yourself – and before you know it you'll be two pounds lighter – then three, then four.

At some stage in all this someone will say, 'Julie, have you lost weight?' and you're on your way.

I deliberately limit any weight-loss regime to fourteen weeks, which means I'm over a stone lighter (or around seven kilos) than when I started. I then focus on maintaining my new weight for a month before deciding whether it's necessary to lose any more.

If you've tried and failed with other systems, why not give it a try? It's only fourteen weeks. By all means email and tell me I'm full of it if you sincerely try my 'program' and it doesn't work for you.

I'm twelve and a half stone (about eighty kilos) at the time of writing this chapter. My target weight is ten stone eleven (about sixty-eight kilos). I'll let you know how I go before the end of this book . . .

10

Middle-Class Madness

One of the inevitable consequences of taking a break from the hamster wheel was endless discussions. Mostly about how laughable it was to ever think I could afford our kids' school fees as a writer. A recent survey found that the average earnings of a published author in Britain are less than a quarter of the national wage. If we assume a similar rule applies to Australia (which is extremely optimistic, as the Australian market is three times smaller than the British one), that means an averagely successful published writer in Australia has the mouth-watering prospect of earning approximately ten thousand dollars a year from sales of their books.

What does that mean for me and my family? Even if I was able to write books that were twice as successful as the average writer's, and produce a new book every year, I'd still have to write a book every year for *sixty years* to afford the bill I am facing for school fees. And that's without paying for anything else – like food or rent or clothes or petrol or, God forbid, a holiday. No, my sixty years of writing would just cover the cost of my kids' education – which is something that the government provides free. Not only do they provide it for free, they do it rather well.

We'd personally had nothing but the most wonderful experiences with the State system. Ignoring the advice of our posher friends, we'd sent all four of our children to the local school. Turned out to be one of the best decisions we ever made. Not once did we feel our kids were losing out in comparison to those who were going to expensive fee-paying schools. And above that it connected the whole family to the local community in a way that I will forever be grateful for. Which makes it all the more bizarre that when it came to high school we decided to send them to fee-paying schools.

I like to think that Kate and I are an intelligent couple but, seriously, why the fuck would we even think of doing something so utterly stupid? Well, as they say in the movies, it's complicated. Much as I'd like to claim I'm a champion of the state school system and my pushy snobby wife forced me into it, the truth is I'm to blame.

My own schooling was sub-optimal to say the least, leaving me with a deep-seated desire to provide the very best educational experience I can for my own kids. So, like a good middle-class lemming, I moronically ignored the example of my own childhood – where 'expensive' had actually meant 'crap' – and embarked on a tour of the private schools of Sydney. I was in a good job at the time and as our eldest was approaching year seven and we'd sent all four of them to the local state school for their primary years, it somehow seemed the natural thing to do. Why? Don't ask me, it just did. Besides, it was only one child we were talking about so what could possibly be the harm?

The first of these visits was a disaster. I'm sure the school in question is actually fine, but the teacher we met on that day spent the entire time we were with him talking about how many prime ministers and Olympic athletes had gone to the school and how the school had a vigorous philosophy of excellence and an 'A stream' policy that worked. We listened to his borderline Aryan rant for forty-five minutes until he finally paused for breath and I asked, 'What about the boys who aren't in the A stream?'

'What do you mean?' he replied, nonplussed.

'You know – those boys who aren't going to make the First XV or excel academically,' I said.

He looked at me, momentarily lost for words, the expression on his face powerfully communicating, 'Why do you ask? Who gives a fuck about *them*?' After a few seconds he pulled himself together and launched enthusiastically into a speech about the excellent system the school had to turn the non-A-streamers *into* A-streamers. The notion that some children simply wouldn't excel didn't seem to exist at this establishment. Forget getting the best out of the child – whatever that might mean in each case. Here it had already been decided that 'the best', for all and everyone, involved playing for the First XV rugby team and/or setting you on the path to become a captain of industry. I left the school feeling thoroughly depressed.

Kate and I had a number of less extreme but similar experiences over the next few weeks. Clearly these schools had worked out their market and realised that guaranteed super-achievement – whether it be in exams, on the sporting field or on the career ladder – was what the aspirational cashed-up parents wanted, so that was what the schools were selling. And much as I'd love all my kids to be super-achievers (albeit *happy* super-achievers), neither Kate nor I see it as the be-all and end-all of a well-rounded quality education.

A month into our tour of the city's 'premier' educational establishments I was actually feeling quite upbeat. If we didn't find a school we liked then we wouldn't have to stump up twenty-five grand a year out of our post-tax income. Not a bad result, was my feeling as we made our way to the last school on our list. Unfortunately, this visit turned out to be even worse than the first. Not because it made me depressed, but because I fell in love.

Call me an old softie, but barely five minutes into the headmaster's speech I was close to tears as he spoke about the type of men they wanted to send out into the world after their time at the school. The sixteen characteristics of a good man as defined by the school included: the positive contribution they make to the world; interacting well with others, particularly women; the life they led; the choices they made.

The headmaster also spoke about sport, but instead of boffing on about the First XV he actually uttered the words: 'At this institution sport exists not for the glory of the school but for the education of the boys.' (It's only fair to point out here that the school has a reputation for continually getting flogged on the field, so a cynic could make a good case that he had to say that.) He talked about his desire to get the best out of each boy – whether that involved becoming a ballet dancer or a special forces commando, a poorly paid social worker or a million-dollar-earning CEO.

Though the headmaster wouldn't have spoken for more than half an hour by the end of it I believed, and still do, every word he said. It was like he was talking directly to my heart. I didn't just want to send my son there, *I* wanted to go there.

After the speech we were taken on a tour of the school by one of the boys – unaccompanied. No teacher there to vet what was said. Admittedly, I was biased by this stage, but the tour only served to strengthen my feeling that I had found precisely what I was after. So I got out the chequebook and joined the waiting list.

It was madness, utter madness. Not because the school has proved to be anything other than what Kate and I hoped for – if anything, it has exceeded our hopes. No, the madness is in not properly and rationally working through the long-term implications of this decision. In my emotional state I worked out in my head that, given my salary at the time, I could comfortably cover the bill for the next year. But obviously it wasn't going to be for one year. Nor for one child. Having sent the eldest to BleedYouDry Grammar it was inevitable we'd feel obliged to keep him there – and then do the same for the other three. In one of my more fiscally frightened moments I did once raise the possibility that maybe we couldn't afford to send all four of them to Eton Towers and perhaps the girls could go to the local school like so many others. I must stress I wasn't thinking in terms of gender – it was purely a numerical argument; it was a chronological accident that numbers three and four happened to be female. Although the scar on my head has now healed you can still clearly see the dent in the saucepan that Kate used to communicate her response.

The thing is, we're not alone. I know many, many people who are in the same boat.

'Nigel, how come there's so much month left at the end of the money?' one such dad asked me recently. I'm not talking here about the wealthy families for whom affording school fees isn't an issue. I'm talking about families who on any rational analysis simply can't afford it. Yet they still send their kids to the expensive schools. And in many cases go into serious crippling debt. Or sign up for decades of living death in multiple jobs they hate to pay for their little loves' schooling. Even though you can get it for free down the road. I'm not criticising, or asking for sympathy, I'm just pointing out that it's madness. Utter madness.

And given my decision to leave my job, we're clearly every bit as mad as the best of them.

11

The Power of None

Writing may be less than useless when it comes to earning a living, but it does have other benefits – one such being the relationship between author and reader. Or, more accurately, the *communication* between author and reader. You see, for the last seven years I have been in the blessed situation of receiving a handful of emails from readers every week. I say 'blessed' because most of the messages are really rather special.

Almost all of the people who email me have read my books and feel like they know me, which, given I expose myself so much in my writing, I suppose they do. This, combined with the fact that they don't expect ever to meet me – another fair assumption – means that some of them write the most amazing, intimate, heartfelt letters. I guess it's because I'm a safe outlet for them. They can write to me about their feelings without any risk of being made to look a fool. Some tell me they hate their jobs, others that they are unhappy with their relationship, and yet others talk about the struggles they have with their parents – and kids. I hear about people's battles with booze, diet disasters, bedroom failures, guilt, fears and secret hopes.

Some recount their triumphs as well – wonderful, uplifting stories of success against the odds and resilience in the face of tragedy. I suspect in many cases I am the only person they can talk to so openly. It's not why I began to write – in fact, I never really anticipated receiving reader letters – but I've come to love it.

To date I've received over ten thousand letters or emails and have replied to every single one. Many write back and we strike up a correspondence; others I've arranged to meet. Some have become friends. One of my sons has even spent a week doing work experience for one of my correspondents. It's like a secret life. On the one side I have the world of macho corporate shenanigans, the politics, the pettiness, the pretence, the posturing, the competitiveness, and on the other is a world of authenticity, humility, openness and kindness. It might be a slightly shocking reflection on the life I lead, but on a number of occasions I've had more meaningful conversations and made deeper connections with total strangers than with people I've known for years.

That's not to say I don't receive any negative feedback. I *especially* enjoy replying to those. One woman wrote, 'You think you're so clever with all your swearing', another that my views on sex were 'awful and medieval', yet another that my grammar was terrible and that 'chuffing' wasn't a real word. Yet in all these cases, after I'd replied they wrote back delightful letters. It's an area of my life where there is no pretence or bullshit. I don't have to put on an act or claim I'm right or that someone else is wrong – I just try to lovingly and authentically say what I feel. And although there isn't a financial payback for writing to readers, there is an enormous emotional one. I learn from each and every conversation I have. I change my position, evolve my thinking, see a different perspective.

At my stage of life I might be expected to have a contracting social circle – a life where the people I interact with become slowly more and more limited and similar as I inevitably settle into a routine of what I know and am comfortable with. Yet, miraculously, my human interaction has exploded. I'm getting letters from people in countries I've never visited, from people who think I'm wonderful and people who think I'm a jerk. Many of these people share an interesting angle on everything from how to successfully balance career and family to how to avoid being injured while running. I find these encounters endlessly fascinating, satisfying and enriching.

Which is why, when readers' emails stopped coming a few months ago, I felt a huge sense of loss. I'd check my inbox every other day and was disappointed, then depressed, when my inbox was empty for the first time in years. As it remained empty week after week, I told myself it was because my books were getting old, that every dog has its day, no one is on top of the mountain forever, and so on. But I couldn't deny that I missed them. The empty inbox exercised a powerful hold on me. Less the power of one, more the power of none. It made me sad when I thought about it.

So it was that one day a speakers' agent called me on my home number.

'Is that Nigel Marsh?' he said.

'Yes,' I replied.

'At *last*. You're a very difficult man to track down.'

'What on earth do you mean?' I asked.

'Well, I've been trying to get hold of you for four weeks.'

'It's not that difficult,' I pointed out. 'My email address is in the back of my books.'

'That's no use to me if you're not going to reply to emails.'

'Reply to what?'

'The emails I send.'

'I haven't received any emails from you.'

'Well I've sent three,' he said, explaining that he'd started to think I was incredibly rude for not even bothering to acknowledge his offer of a speaking job.

I was mortified – not just because I had by now missed the chance to take a job that would cover half an hour of my kids' education, but because it was important to me to reply to everyone and if this speakers' agent's emails hadn't got through, how many other people were out there who I unwittingly hadn't acknowledged?

After I got off the phone, I sent myself an email. It didn't arrive. I asked a friend to do the same. It didn't appear either. Finally I got the IT wizard at work to look into it. Half an hour later, four hundred and eighty-eight emails arrived in my inbox en masse. Apparently there'd been a mix-up with the settings on my Gmail account and all email from my website for the last couple of months had been sitting in a sort of cyber holding bay.

I sat down that evening and read each email, continuing on well into the early hours of the morning. It was one of the most intense and moving nights of my life. I had never had that volume of correspondence in one go. It's difficult to describe, but it was like if your partner collected all the nice things she'd said to you over five years *and told you all over again in one evening*. It was utterly overwhelming and uplifting.

It's been said that the deepest craving of every human being is to be appreciated. At that moment, irrespective of school fees, I wouldn't have swapped those emails for all the money on Wall Street. Of course, after a while I regained my composure and now will happily consider any offers Wall Street cares to make . . .

12

Fuck Off, Lance Armstrong

I don't mean to be rude, but Michael Phelps can fuck off as well. Not, I hasten to add, because either of them have done anything wrong. Quite the reverse – they can fuck off because they have done so much *right*. I have enormous respect for both men's achievements, which are truly remarkable and awe inspiring. Just not particularly helpful – in fact, downright damaging.

I love a tale of super-achievement and triumphing against the odds as much as the next person, but we need to be extremely careful with these stories because, while on the one hand they entertain and inform us, on the other they can demotivate and mislead. Let's be honest, most of us are never going to triumph seven times in the Tour de France or win eight gold medals at an Olympic Games. Reading about people who do to inspire yourself can, unfortunately, have precisely the opposite effect to the one you were hoping for. Why get up early and go for a twenty-five minute swim in the cold when your objective is something as comparatively pathetic as completing a one-kilometre ocean race in six months' time?

I have come to believe I can learn more from happy average achievers than from exceptional overachievers. I don't want to know how to win at the Olympics; I want to know how to get and stay in recognisable shape while maintaining a meaningful marriage and raising four kids. I also want to learn how to maintain a regime over the long term and enjoy it as I go.

I believe we need to make moderate and sustainable achievement heroic. Losing a pound a week for fourteen weeks and keeping it off for a year *is* heroic – especially if you're a single mum working two jobs. In many ways, doing something like this can be your own personal Everest climb or Olympic gold medal. Training to do a ten-kilometre fun run and completing it smiling and uninjured and then continuing to jog twice a week for the year after the race is heroic. We need to change our focus. I want to know more about people who've cracked the code of sustainable enjoyable improvement and less about ultramarathoners who've completed sixty marathons in sixty days (impressive though that is). I want to learn and improve so I can lead a better life overall, not so I can get in *The Guinness Book of Records*. I want to be able to identify with my heroes. Lance and Michael are *too* good, their achievements too grand, their regimes too extreme. They also never seem to fall victim to natural grubby human weakness.

Anyway, back to my resolution to lose a pound a week. A fortnight after setting this goal for myself, I was staying in a hotel in Melbourne. Sure enough, I ate a chocolate bar out of the minibar. Then another. Fuck it, I thought, I've lapsed now so I might as well get some treats in while I'm at it. So I ordered a bowl of ice cream from room service. While I waited for it to arrive, I ate a packet of peanuts and a packet of crisps from the minibar. To finish the evening off with a flourish I lay in bed with a can of Coke and a bag of lollies and watched David Letterman.

The next morning I had my normal 'diet breakfast' of a healthy bowl of muesli, some orange juice and a bit of wholemeal toast. After that I couldn't resist a full cooked breakfast.

On the plane home that morning I was offered another breakfast and heard myself say, 'Yes please.' Three breakfasts down, after I landed in Sydney I bought a Cadbury Creme Egg from a newsagent (I have no idea why, I hadn't eaten one for over twenty years) and a pack of wine gums. I finished them both on the short taxi ride home – just in time for Kate to whisk me out for a welcome-home lunch down at the beach. That week I didn't lose one pound – I *put on four*. I'm not sure how much of a meaningful conversation I could have with Lance and Michael about this. My friend Thomas, on the other hand, understands precisely because she's done her own version of my Melbourne Blowout many times before.

That's not to say extreme achievers haven't got their uses. They show us what humans are truly capable of and can improve society generally through the effects of their deeds. Just as the poor soul who threw herself under a horse helped get women the vote, trailblazers can make breakthroughs that we all benefit from. But apart from major societal changes, I just feel we need to keep a sense of perspective about the reality of their usefulness for the rest of us in everyday life.

13

Pick a Number

My aversion to chasing extreme sporting goals means when I go for a run I tend to do so immensely slowly. One of the advantages of this approach is that it gives me a wonderful opportunity to reflect. As I happily trundle along admiring the gorgeous coastal scenery and being overtaken by people twice my age, my mind goes to work. Sometimes I deliberately focus on a particular issue that needs attention, like a challenge one of my kids is struggling with. Other times I let my mind wander wherever it wants to go. I set out knowing exactly where my legs will take me, but having no clue where my thoughts will end up. Often I mentally travel to the most unlikely and bizarre places. My musings take me both forward into an imagined future and back to revisit events in the past. There doesn't seem to be any rhyme or reason as to which way it goes, but I never fail to find it an illuminating – if not always enjoyable – experience.

In the months after our trip to England my thoughts were inevitably drawn towards the question of how on earth the family would survive financially when my last day in the office arrived.

This was not an entirely comfortable process because, as with previous breaks I had taken, I was *deliberately* determined not to work through the practical realities of our situation. This may sound irresponsible or foolish (Kate maintains it doesn't just *sound* it – it *is* irresponsible and foolish) but I beg to disagree. I knew full well that if I did work through the detailed implications of my decision to leave conventional work I would arrive at the unavoidable conclusion that I shouldn't be doing it. *But I have a firm belief that if you wait until you have satisfied all possible objections to a potential course of action before you embark on it, more often than not you'll never start.* I'm not advocating being stupid, but thousands of us are held back from living the lives we dream of because we feel we have to have all the answers in advance. In fact, a case could be made that nothing worthwhile would ever be achieved if everyone followed this approach. After all, when Columbus set sail he didn't have an answer to every foreseeable problem that could arise during the voyage – what he had instead was an idea he was passionate about. Sometimes you have to follow your heart and trust you'll be able to deal with the challenges as they arise. Well, that's my theory and I'm sticking to it.

But it wasn't just financial musings that had the capacity to make my runs uncomfortable. On a recent outing I set out jogging full of the joys of life with a huge smile on my face when suddenly – bam! – I was hit from nowhere by an enormous wave of guilt, embarrassment and regret as I remembered a weekend Kate and I had spent in Adelaide five years ago. Feeling like a rare break, we arranged a couple of days in South Australia without the kids. On the first night we decided to throw caution to the wind and visit the Adelaide casino. We hardly ever gamble – as a couple we'd only ever been to a casino twice before – but the idea just grabbed us, so we skipped dinner and set aside the amount we would have spent in a restaurant for our night's gambling. If we lost we'd be no worse off than if we'd eaten and if we won . . . well, we'd have won.

Just before we left the hotel I called my mum in England.

'Hi Mum, it's Nigel.'

'Hello,' she replied with what I thought was a slightly frosty tone.

'Kate and I are in Adelaide and we're about to go to the casino.'

'Yes?'

'Well I wondered if you'd like to pick some numbers.'

'What do you mean?' she asked.

'Some numbers. We could bet on them for you.'

'Alright then: nine,' she replied.

'Oh. Are you sure? Would you like any others?'

'No, just nine.'

As Mum was clearly in no mood for a chat I said my goodbyes, told her I loved her, then hung up.

'Mum was in a bit of a strange mood,' I said to Kate.

'Really? What numbers did she choose?' Kate asked.

'She only wanted one – nine,' I replied. And then it hit me. 'Oh, arsing hell.' I yelled in anguish. 'Bollocksing bollocksing arsing hell!'

'Jesus, Nigel, what's wrong?'

'The ninth of August is her *birthday*,' I wailed. 'It was last week and I've missed it. Again.' I sank down on the edge of the hotel bed with my head in my hands. It was the second year in a row that I'd forgotten my darling mum's birthday. It's not like I have many to remember; Dad's incapacitated and I only have one brother. How could I be such an uncaring, thoughtless idiot? Mum lived alone so for her to go through her entire birthday without receiving a card or even a call from her younger son must have been deeply hurtful. And I had no excuse. None.

I called her back and apologised and wished her a happy birthday belatedly, but it was awful. Naturally, Mum was upset.

'It makes it abundantly clear where I fit in your priorities, Nigel,' she said.

None of my protestations that I loved her dearly and that I called her every week and that birthdays just weren't that important to me could change the fact that actions speak louder than words and I had forgotten.

Remembering this as I jogged slowly back home along the coast path I relived all over again the shame and self-loathing

I felt on that day. The proverb that the worst curse of old age is ungrateful children seemed to apply directly to me.

Then again, sometimes it's obedient children who cause you the most angst. The last time I had felt this bad was when Harry was three years old and we were on a trip to the local council pool. It was in my drinking days and I was nursing the mother of all hangovers. Half an hour after we arrived Harry came over to where I was lying in the shade, looked me in the face with his gorgeous innocent eyes and asked, 'Daddy, can I go for a wee in the pool?'

My head was thumping with the after-effects of the previous night's overindulgence. I could see the toilets were at the far end of the sporting complex and I didn't want to leave the shade. So, to my eternal shame, I answered in the affirmative.

'Yes. Just this once, mate,' I whispered.

As I watched him run to the pool I felt a wave of love. He was so cute. He reminded me of Mowgli out of *The Jungle Book*. Just an adorable innocent bundle of energy and wonder. But to my horror, when he reached the edge of the pool he didn't jump into it like he'd been doing all afternoon. No, this time he stood at the edge, pulled his swimming trunks down to his knees and proceeded to urinate into the deep end in an impressive arc. A swimmer who narrowly missed a face full of three-year-old's pee shouted at him to stop. A middle-aged mum ran over to angrily remonstrate with him. I got to him just in time for him to point at me and tearfully – and loudly – explain to the lifeguard and the assembled throng, 'But Daddy said I could wee in the pool.'

Brilliant.

However inexcusable my behaviour was on that afternoon, my crime with Mum's birthday was far worse – especially given Dad's situation. If I found his illness upsetting I could only imagine how appallingly distressing it must be for Mum. After forty-five years of marriage she didn't deserve to have her life partner taken from her in such a cruel and ongoingly painful way. Amazingly, she never complained, always stoically putting on a brave face, refusing to be a burden to anyone. The least she could expect in such circumstances was the love and support of her two sons. I consoled myself with the fact that at least my elder brother Jonathon more than upheld his end of the bargain.

When I got home from my run I checked for the hundredth time that the ninth of August was written in every diary, iPhone, computer and kitchen notepad we possessed. The fact that it was made me feel slightly, but not much, better. One of the many reasons I wanted to leave my job was so I could spend time and effort improving the quality of my human connections. Making sure I'd remember my mum's birthday seemed such a depressingly basic place to start that it made me realise just how much work I needed to do in that area. My run that day might not have done much for my fitness, but it sure as hell gave me a good moral workout.

14

Shuford2000

Despite my own appalling behaviour regarding my mum, I'm an optimist when it comes to human nature. Or, more accurately, a long-range collective optimist. Notwithstanding all the atrocities and failures throughout the ages, on the whole I think history demonstrates that, as a species, we tend to make things better over the generations. It may have taken us a while, but we eventually abolished slavery, eradicated many diseases and gave women the vote. I choose to believe we'll get round to sorting out the environment, terrorism and the growing disparity between rich and poor as well. Maybe not in my lifetime, but we will do it.

It was within this context that I started thinking about the dramatic developments in information technology over recent years. The media and methods of communication have changed beyond all recognition in my lifetime. I remember when there was only one commercial channel and even that didn't broadcast all day. And for a lot of my life a daily newspaper was *the* way of accessing important breaking news and comment. Now it would seem positively quaint to turn to paper and ink to find out the result of a political election or sporting fixture. Why wait twenty-four hours for out-of-date news when you can click a button on your computer and get live feeds on anything you could possibly want to know?

It's no exaggeration to say my children might *never* buy a newspaper. Why would they? The choice and access out there is mind-boggling. And it's 'democratic'. No longer is information the privilege of the lucky few. If you're connected to the internet you have as much knowledge at your fingertips in the poorest, most remote African village as you do in downtown New York. Truly wonderful, transformative progress for humanity.

But, as with everything in life, this has its drawbacks – none more depressing than the rise of the 'comment board'. I'm all for people having a forum to express themselves, but am not convinced that the increasingly ubiquitous comment sections are the best way of achieving this. In days gone by when, say, a painting was hung in a gallery no one put a whiteboard and pen underneath it so visitors could write their opinion of it for all to see. You wouldn't expect to see *Mona Lisa* with 'This painting is shit and the artist is a right wanker' displayed underneath it. People would examine the work, then express their opinions to their circle of friends and family.

Now, whenever you produce something, immediately next to it is the wit and wisdom of anyone who cares to pass comment.

You don't just read an article or view a video online, you read it and at the same time are also exposed to the eight hundred and fifty-eight comments below from people who don't even have to possess any expertise in the particular area concerned or have to justify their opinion. They can just say whatever they feel at the time and can choose to do so anonymously – and anonymous comment boards hardly encourage measured and balanced views.

Last year I was lucky enough to be asked to speak at a TED conference. I spoke about work–life balance and acquitted myself satisfactorily, even managing to generate a modicum of positive feedback (www.ted.com/talks/nigel_marsh_how_to_make_work_life_balance_work.html). The speeches are all posted on YouTube so, if you're interested, you can track the popularity of your speech by the number of views it gets. Moreover, the helpful people at Google will also tell you at a click of a button who has viewed your speech, when and from where. All quite exciting if you seem to have touched a chord and your speech is spreading by word of mouth.

After a few weeks my views were more than fifty thousand and climbing steadily. It had become a guilty secret part of my morning routine to sit down at my desk with a cup of coffee and click on YouTube to see the latest number. Pure vanity, I shamefacedly admit. I'd also scroll down to read the messages left on the comment board, as people were being rather generous and kind. All in all, a pleasant way to start the day – until the morning I got a rude shock instead of my expected warm glow. There was the latest comment for all to see: 'You are all idiots. This guy is a professional conman. You think he cares about work–life balance? Try working for the prick.' It was signed 'Shuford2000'.

I was crushed. On one level it's rather funny and served me right for looking for affirmation on a website. But on a personal level I felt deeply hurt. Much as I tried to put it out of my mind, I spent most of the day wondering who Shuford2000 was. A friend supportively told me that there are people called 'trolls' who spend their time randomly leaving abusive remarks on internet comment boards. For the hell of it, because they can. She pointed me to a number of sites where people had written the most awful things about the most admirable of people. But still I wasn't convinced. It just didn't come across as a random troll piece of abuse – I wasn't well known enough to attract that type of attention. It read like someone who either worked for me or had recently done so. Another friend pointed out we'd just been through the GFC and, given I'd had to make a large number of people redundant, it was most likely someone I'd had to let go who held a grudge. Again, a reasonable suggestion, but still it didn't help.

When I was a young man starting out in my career we'd all pile into the pub at the end of the working day, get drunk and, if the mood took us, slag off the boss. Nothing wrong with that – it goes with the territory of being a boss. Yet those comments never used to leave the pub or be heard by a broader audience – nor were they permanently left on display. In today's media and communications landscape if you want to put yourself forward in any way – whether it be taking a leadership position or producing something creative – you'll need to develop a rhino-thick skin because you'll inevitably end up reading horrible things about yourself or your work.

None of these musings helped. I wanted to talk to Shuford2000 and hear his (assuming for the moment it was a bloke) point of view – and change his mind if I could. Still do in fact. Maybe he had a legitimate grievance I need to apologise for and learn from. Or maybe he was motivated by cowardly, mischievous spite. It's impossible to tell from a short anonymous message. So if you're reading this, Shuford2000, please get in touch. Seriously. I would like to meet you. I'll stand you a breakfast by the beach – even if we end up agreeing to disagree.

•

The reason I was so hurt by dear old Shuford is that he went to the heart of an issue that is very important to me. If he had said I was ugly or boring or stupid I like to think I wouldn't have given it too much thought. But the comment posted included the question: 'Do you think he cares about work–life balance?' Well yes, actually, I do. So much so that I've written two books about it, resigned twice from highly paid jobs mid-career and wiped out the family's savings to spend significant slugs of time with my family and was about to do it again for a third time. Hardly the behaviour of someone who doesn't care about it.

More importantly, however, I don't just care about work–life balance for me – I care about it for other people. Especially when I'm in some way responsible for them.

I'm lucky enough to have had a number of senior leadership roles in my career. Some of those roles involved running companies with hundreds of employees. In each of those roles I've carried a dog-eared St Augustine quote on me, picked up from my years studying theology at university, which says: 'It is immoral to misuse people, underuse them and abuse them, but it is highly moral to call forth and make use of the talents that are in people. It is also certain that people will not use their gifts to the benefit of the organisation unless they are treated as people, with all the needs people have.' Beautiful.

These words may have been uttered by St Augustine in the fifth century, but they are every bit as profound and relevant hundreds of years later.

I'm not by any means claiming I'm perfect, but I am claiming that I sincerely attempt to be a good boss which, unfortunately, is more than you can say for many – including my first boss. Back then I was working for the railways (not my childhood dream, more a function of the fact that a degree in theology doesn't really qualify you for anything apart from a role in the Church – and the small matter of having no faith was holding me back from that particular path) and the person I directly reported to clearly hated me on sight. Not only that, but he spent every day trying to make my life a living hell. On most days he succeeded. Apart from making me extremely miserable, this had the effect of making me swear that if I ever got into a position of power I would never be a 'bad' boss.

It's difficult to define what being a good or bad boss means but, a bit like sex appeal, you know it when you see it. And I've seen it a lot. A few years ago, I witnessed a worldwide management meeting in America where one particular country manager was being praised to the skies and held up as an example to all the other country managers. The person in question had regularly delivered forty per cent margins in his stint as CEO, while the others were struggling to get their profit into double figures. In the hotel bar after the board meeting I approached the hero CEO.

'Those are pretty amazing results you've delivered,' I said. 'I'd love to know how you do it.'

'It's very simple,' he replied. 'I can tell you in one word.'

'Really? Just one word?'

'Yep – just one word. It's worked for me for ten years and I guarantee it will work for anyone else.'

'I'm all ears – what is it?'

'Slavery,' he replied.

'Pardon?' I said.

'Slavery.'

'Slavery?'

'That's right – slavery. I never pay more than the minimum wage and if anyone so much as looks like they're going to complain or ask for a raise, I fire them on the spot.'

I was appalled but, a bit like not being able to resist the temptation to slow down and glance at a traffic accident, I wanted to know more. I asked for a tour of his offices. They didn't disappoint. Or rather they did. They were exactly what his earlier comments had led me to expect. Hideously overcrowded and clearly in need of some basic upkeep. I quizzed him on turnover rates and morale. He happily confessed that both were what you would expect in a sweatshop. And here's the thing – *he didn't care*. When someone resigned, he simply replaced them. When someone else pointed to the awful morale, he pointed to the profit number. The phrase 'evil genius' sprang to mind.

But there is a profound lesson here. Contrary to what all those supposed management gurus tell you, *being an outright bastard in business works financially*. When presented with this reality the gurus (many of whom have never come within a hundred miles of actually running a company, preferring instead simply to talk about it) counter, 'Ah yes, but in the long term it's more profitable to be nice.' I have two problems with this response. First, they are wrong. The bloke in question had been running his agency like that for ten years – and moreover, some of the most financially successful companies I have worked with have been the ones with the very worst cultures. For example, during the time that Lord King was running British Airways to worldwide acclaim with spectacular long-term results, he was asked, 'How do you motivate your employees?' His simple and unashamed answer was: 'Fear.' Perhaps a step up from 'Slavery', but we're still in 'bad boss' territory, I feel.

My second problem with the gurus' 'it pays to be nice in the long term' theory is a moral one. You should be nice not because it enhances profits in the long term but because it is the right thing to do. Full stop. People are human beings with souls and families and feelings, they're not merely economic units of production. They deserve to be treated with empathy and respect. Do unto others and all that. In many cases being nice may *cost* the firm money over the long term. However it is also even more likely that it will make your firm more successful. 'How so?' I hear the accountants cry. It's all a matter of how you define success.

If we're to define success solely by how much margin can be squeezed out of the business, we're in trouble. If, however, the definition of success includes such things as employee engagement and the long-term viability of the company, then we're in business. At one of the firms I managed I gave everybody two doona days a year where they could stay in bed if they woke up and couldn't be arsed to come to work. At another I gave everyone their birthday off. Did either make the firms in question more profitable? Hell no. Were they good ideas? You bet your life they were. It's a mindset, I suppose. You either think Chainsaw Al Dunlap (see *Chainsaw: The Notorious Career of Al Dunlap in the Era of Profit-at-Any-Price*), who slashed his way through corporate America, was a visionary hero or you think he was a repellent jerk. At the risk of coming off the fence on this one, I think there is a special room in hell for him and his kind.

All of the above is not to say that a good boss has to be what the Australians charmingly call a 'soft cock' (i.e. someone who lets everyone walk all over them and never makes the hard decisions). I'm well aware that the touchy-feely tree-hugging stuff can go too far and create all sorts of problems. Most damagingly, it can lead to unrealistic expectations. Some

employees have hopelessly impractical ideas of what is possible
in the harsh commercial world. Others are breathtakingly
ungrateful and spoilt when it comes to the thoughtful work
conditions their employers have bent over backwards to provide
them with. The business world is complex. Leadership is
difficult. Often impossibly so. No one is perfect. Work is hard.
Firms have to be profitable or else they go out of business and
everyone loses their jobs. How profitable a company needs to
be is the issue. It's all about balance.

And honesty.

And this is where we come to an area of the whole work–life
balance debate that is not often talked about. As I've said
repeatedly in print, it is ultimately up to us as individuals
to design the type of life we want and then to take personal
responsibility for setting and enforcing the barriers that will
let us have that life. It is unfair and naive of us to expect
governments or companies to do it for us.

The trouble in a surprising number of cases isn't a horrible
employer or a harassed father who simply hasn't had the time
or mental space required to design his life. The problem is that
the person in question secretly *wants* a singular, all-consuming
focus on his career. This is rarely spoken of, but is a serious
issue within the work–life balance debate. What is my view
of those people? Fine – it takes all types to make the world
go around – on two conditions. First, you need to be sure it's
a conscious choice and not an unwitting slide into a lifestyle
that gives you a successful career and an old age full of regrets.

Second, you have to make sure your choice isn't detrimental to anyone else you share your life with.

Many men use the office to escape from their families – or, more accurately, the bits they don't enjoy, or are scared of, in their families. I've seen more instances than I care to remember of colleagues delaying their departure from the office so they will arrive home just after the teatime, bathtime, bedtime nightmare has ended, meaning they can get the cuddles without having to endure any of the hard work.

A consultant friend of mine has told me that on more than one occasion a prominent client of his has asked for meetings on a Saturday. When told the work could easily wait until the start of the next working week the reply was: 'No, I want it on Saturday to give me an excuse to get out of the house and escape all the bloody noise.' Tragic but true. And in more cases than I suspect we realise, it is representative of a prevailing view. In many cases it is just too easy to blame the boss or employer when the real issue lies elsewhere. It was a lesson I wanted to be sure to remember during my impending break.

15

Holland versus Germany

While scheduling Saturday meetings 'to escape the noise' is hardly an acceptable excuse for shirking your parental duties, I can understand the sentiment. As any mother will tell you, looking after young kids is no walk in the park. There is also an enormous difference between 'helping with the kids' and having primary care and responsibility for them.

For many men who've dreamt of quitting the rat race and spending more time with their kids, the reality can come as quite a shock. The truth is that childcare can actually be enormously stressful, tiring and thankless. Some male executives don't believe me when I tell them how hard their stay-at-home partners work even though they are not in an office. They seem to think it's all Pilates at the beach and fun times with the ladies who lunch. To help convince them I sometimes ask if they've ever organised for all their far-flung relatives to get together in a holiday house for a family Christmas, the goal being a relaxing week full of joy and laughter? For those who have I ask them to recount how these holidays panned out in reality. After their tales of tears, sulking and tantrums, I point out that if that's what it's like with adults, just imagine what it's like with children.

The trouble is that for many men all the hard work involved in bringing up their children is done for them. That's not to say that they aren't hardworking themselves nor enormously loving fathers. But, a bit like enjoying drinking in a pub gives you no idea how much hard work goes into *running* a pub, enjoying spending time with your kids on the weekend gives you no idea how hard it is to keep them all alive and dressed and safe and entertained and educated and fed and transported and nurtured during the week. It involves relentless grunt work and almost military-precision planning.

It's the last point that's the critical one. The planning. It might work for some, but in the main 'just going with the flow' is a disaster if you want to enjoy being with your kids over any extended period of time. Much as they might enjoy a few days of doing nothing but eating pizza and watching endless TV, it's not a recipe for happiness in the long term.

This is another of the reasons why I continually arrange to do things with my kids. I don't just sign everyone up for community events like races and swims – I invent stuff like the rather morbidly named Life Challenge I launched as I approached my third career break. This was a competition between me and my two sons in which we played tennis and kept a running tally of the score. The basic idea was that the person in the lead when I die wins. I view it as my role to get as many games in now, while they are young enough for me to win, in order to build up a buffer of matches before they get older and start beating me regularly. Given that all the kids can now beat me in swimming races, I clearly haven't got much time left. But it gets us out of the house, gives us a shared focus and provides us with shared experiences.

I read an interesting article recently in which an academic talked about the difference between 'experienced happiness' and 'remembered happiness'. And it turns out the latter is disproportionately important. You may have loved the first ten days of a recent skiing holiday, but if on the last day of that holiday you had a massive row with your wife and one of the kids broke their leg, the chances are that holiday will be ruined forever. You'll carry the lifetime memory of an awful holiday. The academic warned of the dangers of putting too much stock in the remembered type of happiness, suggesting that we live in the moment more.

For me, much as being present in the moment is a great idea, so are collecting and building memories. I'm not advocating that we live in the past, but I do think it's alright to spend *some* time there. Apparently Ghandi once said something like: if you live well you get to enjoy two lives – the actual living of your life and then reliving your life through your memories. As a society we are very quick to advise people to earn and save money for their retirement, but it makes just as much sense to build up and save memories. As you get old and frail, living life reflectively is no bad thing. Thinking about my dad, I dearly hope he had some memory left despite all signs to the contrary. For him and the others in his home it's *all* they've got.

It is possible to fully enjoy the moment and proactively plan to create and store up wonderful memories for the future. There came a stage in my father's illness where he was becoming forgetful and confused and it was clear he wouldn't be able to function normally for much longer. I desperately wanted to get him to one final rugby match before he grew too ill. When I suggested this he wasn't keen initially, as by this stage he found going out stressful. Nevertheless I took him and my boys to a rugby match and made a huge fuss of all three of them, buying them expensive matching team jerseys and making them put them on for the match so we could get a group photo of us all smiling and hugging before kickoff. Much as we all enjoyed the night out, I was primarily doing it because I knew it would be one of the last times we'd be together as a 'normal' family and I wanted a memory for us all to hold dear. I'm looking at the photo now and it brings back waves of remembered happiness. Manufactured? Couldn't care less – it's a damn sight better than picturing him in his current state.

If I could create memories of my parents, I sure as hell want to do it for my kids as well. I'm not a fan of soccer. Never have been. Rugby's my game. However much I try to get into soccer, it simply bores me to tears. But when the FIFA World Cup

Me, Harry, Alex and Dad, Sydney, 2003

was on in South Africa I got the largest tournament wall chart I could find from a newspaper, then cut thirty-two individual bits of paper and wrote a team name on each of them before putting them into a canvas bag.

When I got home that night I got everyone together.

'Right, you lot, I need everyone to go and find one dollar and put it in Family Pig,' I said.

Family Pig is the pink plastic piggy bank we keep in the kitchen for loose change. It has come to play an important part in our family because my standard response to pleas of 'Please, please, please, Daddy, can we have an ice cream?' is 'Only if there's enough money in Family Pig.'

While the kids, Kate and Jan (the friend staying in our spare room at the time) all went off to find their dollars, I stuck the tournament wall chart up in the kitchen. When they returned I explained, 'It's the football World Cup in ten days and we're going to have a family sweepstake.'

'What's a sweepstake, Daddy?' Grace asked.

On that afternoon, like every afternoon for the last two weeks, Grace was wearing a diving mask. The first time she came to the dinner table wearing it I did a double take but didn't say anything. However, when she came home from school and sat down to watch TV with it on I asked in my best non-judgemental voice why she was wearing it. 'Oh, so I'm ready for explosions, Daddy,' was her matter-of-fact reply. Despite the absence of any explosions, it had become such a permanent feature on her face that it no longer seemed strange.

'A sweepstake is where you pick teams and the winner gets a prize.'

'What's the prize? What's the prize?' the twins chorused.

'One hundred dollars,' I said, whipping out two fifty-dollar notes.

Their eyes, even the two behind the diving mask, bulged with amazement. One hundred dollars was an unimaginably huge amount of money to them – especially given they'd just spent five minutes laboriously feeding many five- and ten-cent pieces into the slot in Family Pig's head.

'And if you win,' I added, 'you can spend it on *whatever you like*. All of it.'

'Even sweets?' they asked.

'Even sweets,' I replied.

It would be fair to say I had their attention.

I got everyone to sit down around the dining table and took out the bag with all the teams in it.

'We're going to pick a team, each in turn, and keep going around the circle until there are no more names left in the bag – but first let's take a look at the rankings,' I said, handing out a table of the odds on each team.

'Can I have Spain?' Eve asked as soon as she saw who was on top of the table.

'Nope – you can't choose. You get the team you pick out of this bag.'

There then followed one of the most fun and exciting afternoons I can remember. Each time someone picked a team a cry of joy or groan of disgust would erupt. There was clapping and laughter as the lesser teams were selected. Alex was appalled to pick New Zealand, then North Korea as his first two teams while Grace nonchalantly picked Germany and Argentina as her first two. I was pretty smug about getting Brazil, then Italy. I took the map of the world off the girls' bedroom door to show everyone where some of the less well-known countries were. Jan wrote a name next to every team on a separate chart and we stuck it on the kitchen wall with the rankings next to the tournament match grid.

Dinner that evening was fantastic. The girls were full of questions like 'Do you think Slovakia will win, Daddy?' and 'Can you buy a horse for a hundred dollars?'

And the wonderful thing is that the excitement continued throughout the tournament. In fact, not just continued, but built. Every morning I'd be woken by a ten-year-old girl shaking me excitedly, having got up early to check the scores on the computer. 'Daddy, Daddy, Ghana got a nil–all draw!' she would inform me breathlessly or, more predictably, 'England's goalkeeper let in a sitter.'

We'd get up together in the middle of the night to watch the games, huddled under the same blanket. We'd discuss the results at mealtimes. We'd make a huge drama of crossing names off the list as they got knocked out of the competition. The matches transformed from football teams to family names. Rather than Holland versus Germany it became Harry versus Grace. Or Dad versus Eve. It was heavenly – and, like I said, I don't even like football. It became a marvellous family glue. A shared topic of interest and good-natured joshing. Alex even got his own back as New Zealand played out of their skins and ended the tournament as the only country not to lose a single game. In the end none of the Marshes won as Jan had picked Spain out of the bag. Gorgeously, she divided the money equally between the kids.

Best of all, the joy lasted well beyond the competition itself. Not just as 'remembered happiness', but in its knock-on effect: it led me to take the previously unimaginable step of agreeing to be the assistant coach of the twins' under-10 soccer team. Every Sunday I'd travel to a local park with my friend Errol (the real coach) to stand on the touchline and watch as the Mighty Dragons chased the ball around the pitch like iron filings stuck to a magnet. Despite never having played the game – or, indeed, even knowing the rules – I threw myself into the role with gusto. It soon became one of the favourite parts of my week and resulted in one memory I will cherish well into my old age.

It came out of the blue on an otherwise unremarkable Wednesday as I was sitting at my desk writing. The phone kept on ringing and eventually I succumbed to the temptation that plagues most authors – the natural desire to use any distraction as an excuse to interrupt your writing – and picked up the receiver.

'Hello?' I said.

'Hi, could I speak to Mr Marsh please?' said a pleasant female voice.

'Speaking.'

'It's Melissa here. We'd like to send a photographer to your house – today or tomorrow if possible – and wanted to ask if you could make sure your twins were available to be in it.'

'I'm sorry, who did you say you are?' I asked.

'Melissa. From the *Wentworth Courier*. We'd like to get a photo of you with your girls for next week's paper.'

'Why on earth would you want to do that?' I asked.

'Oh – don't you know? Because of the letter.'

'What letter?'

'The letter your twins sent the paper.'

She went on to explain that Grace and Eve had sent the local paper an email entering me into their Father of the Year competition.

I didn't believe her at first – until she sent me a copy of the email.

I quote: 'My father never gives up he is the best. He is my inspiration the president of own little nation dad has a big happy hart and pulls me along in life's cart. When dad has a great idea he will never give up till the world hears about it. When he says he will do something he will. He reads us stories, takes us to the park, he will always help you if you ask him to he will take us to see our cosins grandma and grandpa and all our relitivs even it if is really expensive.'

While the spelling and grammar weren't perfect, nor the evidence of me whining over the cost of plane tickets flattering, I was stunned. Tearful, if truth be told. Turns out the twins had snuck on to Kate's computer and entered me in the competition one afternoon, having seen an article about it on the front cover of the local newspaper. Although the phrase about 'life's cart' looked suspiciously similar to a poem in a Mother's Day card I'd got them to sign recently, I was touched beyond words. If even half of what they said was true I was happy. The fact that they *thought* it was true made me ecstatic. This was precisely why I'd decided to take another break from the corporate world. It was also perfect timing. It was just the type of affirmation I needed to keep me committed to my decision in the face of financial evidence suggesting it wasn't such a good idea.

Just two days later, while I was still basking in a 'Father of the Year' glow, I received another piece of surprising feedback as I was getting the twins ready for their swimming lesson. Every week they had an argument about who got to wear which pair of goggles and this day was no different. Though I'd tried everything to stop it happening nothing was effective – no matter how many pairs of goggles I bought, whose name I wrote on what pair, and irrespective of any schedule I drew up, each week they'd bicker over them. On this particular day the bickering quickly descended into screaming, then foot-stamping and finally hair-pulling.

'Bloody hell, shut up! I can't stand this!' I shouted. 'And now you've made us late.'

Startled, the twins stopped fighting and fell silent. Standing next to each other in identical swimming costumes they looked up at me with their huge beautiful trusting eyes. If you hadn't witnessed the previous five minutes you would swear butter wouldn't melt in their mouths.

Butter might not melt, but my heart did. Lowering my voice, I knelt in front of them and said, 'Sorry to shout, but you two would test the patience of the Pope. What am I going to do with you?'

'Well, Daddy, you could put us up for adoption and Lisa could adopt us,' Eve suggested without hesitation.

Much as I'm thrilled that our good friend Lisa has such a wonderful relationship with my daughters, the fact that Eve had clearly thought it through and regarded swapping families as a valid option did rather suggest I had a fair way to go before I could legitimately claim any Father of the Year accolade . . .

16

Hits the Spot

Father of the Year or not, I was keen to spend more time with the kids, but while I was still doing my handover at work this was proving difficult during the week. Having found a successor to run the company my mind was increasingly focused on domestic and not commercial matters, but the reality of my daily routine had changed little because I was still having to go into the office every day. I looked forward to the time when I was officially and formally free to spend my time precisely where and how I liked. They say time is money, but I disagree. Time is *everything*.

During this interim period an important anniversary came around. Every year on 5 April I celebrate my alternative birthday.

On 5 April 2003 I gave up drinking and I haven't touched a drop since. I'd come to the conclusion that if I was to be the type of man, husband, father and friend I wanted to be, I'd reached the end of the road alcohol-wise.

Eight years is a long time and I'm proud that I've been able to follow through on my decision to completely cut out the booze. That said, I don't take recovery for granted – nor has it been easy. Throughout those eight years there have been many challenges. Not only have I had to face down some of my own demons, I've also had to learn how to effectively adapt to some of the, ahem, 'quirky' behaviour of other people. And though Kate has put up with more and done more to help me than anyone else on the planet, when it comes to drink she has a slight blind spot.

Let me be clear: Kate was remarkably supportive of my decision to give up alcohol and never once made me feel bad. Nor has she encouraged me to have 'just the one'. For that I will be forever grateful. It's when it comes to her own drinking that things become a little more problematic. It's not so much the drinking itself – it's preparing her drink and then having to watch her drink it that I find a challenge.

Kate's drink of choice is vodka and tonic. She likes it made long, over ice, with a couple of decent squeezes of grapefruit juice.

On one particular evening, as soon as I got through the door Kate yelled from the bathroom, 'Nigel, I'm washing the kids' hair before tea, then helping Eve and Grace with their school project. Could you fix me a drink?'

'Sure,' I replied.

'Good boy. Could you please fix me a drink and then get the washing out of the machine and put another load on before you go to get Alex? He needs picking up at 7.30.'

'Sure. What do you want to drink?' I asked.

'A nice cold long vodka and tonic please. There's a bottle in the freezer.'

I went to the freezer and found the bottle of vodka.

I put four ice cubes in a tall glass and poured the vodka over them so they made that wonderful 'crackling ice' sound. Then I opened a bottle of tonic. The *pzsss* sound and effervescent bubbles reminded me of all those wonderful thirst-quenching Schweppervescence TV commercials I'd grown up with. The ice clinked enticingly as I stirred the glass.

Kate came into the kitchen with a towel over both shoulders, a nit comb in one hand and a school exercise book in the other. She looked longingly at the glass and said, 'Don't forget the grapefruit. There's a freshly cut half by the bread bin. I'll be downstairs combing the twins' hair.'

I located the grapefruit and duly added two good squeezes to the vodka and tonic. The cloudy effect as the juice slowly melded with the rest of the liquid was strangely attractive. Even if I did say so myself, it looked a rather fine drink. I added an extra squeeze for luck and gave the mixture a final stir.

'Hurry up sweetheart. I'm dying of thirst down here. Who's a girl got to shag in this house to get a drink?' Kate shouted up the stairs.

'Just a sec – coming,' I yelled back.

Kate looked like she was going to inhale the thing, not drink it.

I handed her the glass and she took a deep slug with her eyes closed, then opened her eyes and smacked her lips. 'God that hits the spot, Nigel. You may be an irritating bastard on many levels but you don't half make a decent drink. That is about the most perfect vodka I've ever tasted.'

Marvellous. But I couldn't help thinking it was about time I revisited AA.

I don't go regularly to AA. But every now and then when I feel the need to remind myself why I've given up alcohol, or when the call of the vodka bottle is just that little bit louder than usual, I pay a visit. I know people who've been more times in a month than I've been in eight years. Indeed there are those who go once or twice a day every day for the first ninety days of their sobriety. It makes my handful of visits each year look fairly non-committal. And it's true I don't do AA 'properly'. I don't work the steps and have never had a sponsor. On the other hand, the only qualification you need to attend is a sincere desire never to pick up another drink and on that basis I most definitely *do* qualify.

Whether I do it properly or not, I find AA to be the most amazing of organisations. Loving, hardworking, non-judgemental – AA is that rare thing: an institution that is a genuine force for good in our society. Around the world they save lives every day. They are entirely not for profit, welcome everyone and never publicise their good works. Instead they just quietly go about their business helping people to improve their lives.

I'd class my visits to AA as some of the most important occasions in my life because I never fail to be inspired, touched and humbled. The central part of an AA meeting is for members of the group to share their experience of how alcohol has affected their lives and how they have dealt with it. As I listen to people's stories I can feel the good in me rise up and the bad being suppressed. It's no exaggeration to say that after each meeting I leave determined to strive to make the most of my life and be a better person.

Because of my infrequent attendance I don't like to share. I can never quite rid myself of the feeling that I'm a fraud because my story isn't 'bad enough' and my commitment to their program isn't 'good enough'. However, being a well-brought-up lad I don't like to be rude, so when the meeting is small and I'm asked if I'd like to share I find my natural 'be a good guest' syndrome kicks in. After I've introduced myself and said how long I've been sober, I always explain that I'm extremely grateful to the group and find the meetings very valuable but then inevitably end up apologising for the fact that I don't attend very often or do the twelve steps.

Everyone had always been remarkably supportive and understanding until the meeting I went to a couple of months after my last day at the office. I'd given my normal spiel when afterwards, while I was having a cup of tea, an attractive middle-aged woman came up to me.

'It's Nigel, isn't it?' she said.

'Yep,' I replied, offering her my hand.

She can't have seen it because, rather than shaking it, she asked, 'You've not got a sponsor?'

'No.'

'Ever had one?'

'Er, no,' I replied.

'And you've kept off the booze for eight years?'

'Eight years and three months as of tomorrow morning.'

'And you've never worked the steps?'

'No.'

'So you just do it with willpower?' she asked, slightly aggressively.

'Well, that and the support of my family,' I replied, thinking it best not to mention anything about the nightly vodka-and-tonic routine.

'You must be burning up inside keeping it all bottled in like that,' she said.

'Er, without in any way wanting to sound complacent I'm finding it a little easier as the years go by,' I said.

'No, no, you'll be burning up inside,' she insisted. 'You'll get cancer.'

'Pardon?'

'You'll get cancer. If you don't work the steps you'll get cancer.'

'Er . . .'

'Look, I'm telling you you're not addressing the core issue if you don't do the steps. You need to get yourself a sponsor and get them to work through each step with you.'

I truly didn't know what to say. Or think. She was either mad or fanatical, or both. Or maybe she was simply a desperate sponsor on a particularly aggressive recruitment drive.

Either way, as a form of helpful support I'd put it right up there with being asked to make a vodka and tonic.

17

Wedding Cake island

Cancer-threatening nutters aside, my battle with the booze was progressing quite satisfyingly – it was my battle with the bulge that was the more pressing issue.

My last official day in the office had finally come and gone so I was now fully free to focus on my own priorities, but despite my good intentions and mental preparation I'd failed regarding my weight. After nine back-to-back weeks of a pound a week weight loss I'd pigged out on chocolate and ice cream on the weekend and lost my momentum. Maddeningly, I was back to where I started. How come it takes so long to get the weight off and no time at all to put it on? Nine weeks to lose nine pounds – two weeks to put them back on. I'd like to meet the joker who invented that rule.

I was still passionately committed to my weight-loss goal of ten stone eleven pounds as well as unshakeable on my three pillars – patience, delaying gratification and honesty. It was the motivation part I was falling down on. The first time I lost lots of weight it was a central part of a broader midlife-crisis transformation, so I had added incentive to succeed. This time there was no natural added motivation. If I was to achieve my goal I clearly needed to create some. And so I decided to create another three pillars to go alongside the initial three, the first of which would be my hitherto secret and useless obsession with numbers.

All my life I have been interested in numbers. Not mathematical or economic numbers. Date numbers. Or, more accurately, the coincidences and patterns that the numbers of the date throw up. For most people 20 January 2001 was just another day, but for me it was special because it read 20.01.2001. Likewise 8 August 2008. And 2 February 2002 was even better – 02.02.02 being an all-time favourite of mine. The numbers of dates was simply something that had always caught my eye. I noticed when the date added up to thirteen (a bad thing) and when it added up to seventeen (my birthday – a good thing). Depending on how you use the numbers themselves you can almost always invent some sort of relevance, pattern or connection out of the eight numbers of the date. I'm totally flexible. If it helps to include all the numbers, fine. But if leaving off the millennium and century will turn an otherwise boring and unremarkable 10 October 2010 into a (for me) thrilling 10.10.10, then I'm happy to do so. Not a particularly admirable or noble hobby, I realise, which is why I have always kept it to myself. I dread to think what a therapist would say it reveals about my personality.

For years I thought I was alone in suffering from this (hopefully) mild obsessive-compulsive mental flaw, then a couple of years ago I was sent one of those nutty emails about the September 11 terrorist attacks and the importance of the number eleven. Some fruit loop was emailing the world asking everyone to pray for eleven seconds for those in need because the attacks revealed the significance of that particular number. As the email went on to explain, the date of the attack was 9/11 and 9 + 1 + 1 = 11. September 11 is the two hundred and fifty-fourth day of the year – 2+5+4 = 11. After September 11 there are one hundred and eleven days left to the end of the year. And so it went on. Total rubbish, of course, as you can create coincidences out of anything if you go looking for them. But that's the point – that is precisely what I'd been doing for as long as I could remember. The email made me realise how stupid the whole number thing was, but also made me realise that I wasn't alone and at least one other person played the same numerical mind games. Tragic though it might be to find reassurance in the ravings of a lunatic email spammer, from that day on I felt somehow slightly more normal. I decided I was going to use my date obsession for positive ends. I would link it with my weight target and thereby create a specific goal that I had to meet if I was to be true to the significance of the numbers. Hopefully this would put my 'sickness' to good use. After all, I created these connections in my mind and they genuinely meant something to me, so it would be unthinkable for me not to meet my target.

It was a moment of great impact, therefore, when I weighed myself on the morning of 11 August and discovered I weighed eleven stone eight pounds. No big deal unless you're a numbers freak . . . I was *11/8 on 11/8*. Hugely significant and the perfect starting point to losing a pound a week, because if I did so I would be ten stone eleven on 10 November – which for all you non-numbers freaks out there means I would be *10/11 on 10/11*. In my twisted numbers world this was the equivalent of Halley's Comet coming around twice in an afternoon. The dates were sending me a sign as sure as if they'd posted me a letter.

My second new pillar was to link the goal to significant communal events. Those races and swims I sign the family up for could be put to use, just like my number obsession. Every year I try to run the City to Surf from the centre of Sydney to the world-famous Bondi Beach. It's the world's largest timed road race – bigger than the London and New York marathons put together. Call me a sentimental old fool, but it is always one of the happiest days of my life. I approach it with a total lack of cynicism and savour every moment of the day. This year Grace and Eve were joining us in the run for the first time. I decided that the start of my new weight goal would not only be marked by 11/8 but also by the City to Surf race – the fortieth such race and the first for our ten-year-old twins. Of course every goal needs an end, not just a beginning, and the sporting calendar happily presented the perfect such occasion.

Three months after the City to Surf, and a few days after 10/11, the Coogee to Wedding Cake Island Swim takes place. This classic rough-water ocean swim is a good two and a half kilometres. Ever since I did the Bondi to Bronte ocean race it was the next one on my list to conquer, but I'd never found the time, or courage, to attempt it. Until now. I decided my new weight journey was not only '11.8 to 10.11', it was also going to be 'City to Surf to Wedding Cake Island'.

The third extra pillar, however, was perhaps the most important of all.

People.

Other people.

In my professional career I've always believed in great groups not great individuals. Yet in my personal life I incline towards being a bit of a loner, especially when it comes to self-improvement. I'm quite self-reliant and pride myself on my determination as a self-motivator. However, when I look back on my life, most of my successful achievements have been because of the help of other people. Sure, I could kid myself that I and I alone gave up drinking and smoking, but in both of those cases I didn't really do it alone. I may have set the goals, but other people helped me to reach them. Same with getting fit. And learning to swim. In fact, the more I thought of it the more obvious it became. 'No man is an island' may be a cliché, but if I was going to swim around one at my ideal weight I reckoned I needed to take heed of its essential truth.

But which people? I'm allergic to most experts and self-help gurus. In my experience they can tend to spout self-serving rubbish, either talking in lazy platitudes or giving completely impractical advice that no normal person could ever hope to follow. Which is usually the point, repeat custom being the key to these people's vast fortunes. And as I've already pointed out, comparing yourself to super-achievers is a losing game.

So, much as I hate the terms 'normal' or 'real', I wanted some normal real people to join me on my quest. At work I was forever banging on about how anything can be achieved if we create a common sense of endeavour towards a worthwhile goal. Well, now was the time to use that philosophy at home – getting in shape being every bit as worthy as making yet more profits for people overseas that you'd never met.

Enter Louise, Thomas and Steven. Three friends who are quite the loveliest people you could ever hope to meet. Very different in many ways, but similar in one – they all wanted to lose weight and had struggled repeatedly in the past to do so successfully. As a team we were a varied bunch. Two men, two women. Aged from thirty-eight to fifty-eight. Each of us parents of multiple kids. Professions as varied as jewellery design, publishing and film-making. The four of us agreed that we would sign up for, and support each other on, the City to Surf to Wedding Cake Island journey. The only rule was we had to email each other every Monday with our honest weight. The hope was that the collective spirit would then kick in and laggards would be encouraged while those on track would be cheered and congratulated. To mark our commitment we all had our pictures taken at the finish line of the City to Surf run and decided that the next time we'd have a group photo it would be on the beach at the finish line of the Wedding Cake Island swim. After all, there's nothing like a cossie picture to keep you honest.

So with six pillars to bolster me now, rather than three, I confidently took Kate away for the weekend to celebrate our wedding anniversary – and promptly put on three pounds in my first two days. There's many a slip 'twixt the cup and the lip, as someone wiser than me once said.

18

The Magnificent Seven

My aversion to experts has been forged over a twenty-five-year corporate career. Not because of the people I have worked with – I've been blessed in that regard. No, it's because of the books I've read over those years. I've always been a voracious reader. As a young man I used to read at least one book a week and even at the height of career stress I'd always get through at least one a month. I read all sorts of books – novels, history, biographies, the classics, self-help titles, sports books and spiritual tomes. Any book that naturally grabs my interest, or is recommended to me by someone I trust, is eagerly devoured. I usually read in bed last thing at night and my bedside table boasts two teetering piles of as-yet-unread books – forty-five of them at last count.

Because I realised early on that my reading interests and my chosen career were unlikely to naturally overlap I promised myself that I would read a business book between each book I genuinely wanted to read. My reasoning was that this would mean I was up to date with the latest thinking in my industry and business in general, and would therefore help me converse intelligently with my clients. So, remarkable as it may sound, almost without exception every other book I've read over the last twenty years has been a business book. Which is a lot of business books.

And here's the thing. After sober reflection on these books, the fairest conclusion I can come to is . . . most of them are crap. A total waste of time and money. I tried to suppress this creeping realisation during my career but, still, whenever I saw the latest hit title – such as *Who Moved My Cheese?* – I just couldn't help thinking, 'Who's moved your cheese? Who gives a fuck?'

You may ask why I didn't just give up with this 'every other book' rule, but a promise is a promise and it did deliver rather well on its original objective – I was always up to date with the business books that everyone else was talking about.

So what is my problem with this genre? Twofold basically.

First there are simply so many of the damned things. Visit any airport bookshop and there are literally hundreds of business titles. Type 'business success' into Amazon and you get results for more than forty-six thousand titles. And every week brings scores of new releases. It just seems obvious to me that they can't all have discovered the secret to business success. There simply has to be a huge element of overlap, repetition and platitudinous waffle. I'm well aware they wouldn't be published if there wasn't a market for them, but it does all feel a little uncomfortably like the diet book industry. No matter that the diet books clearly don't work, people keep churning them out because there is an insatiable appetite for them anyway.

I understand, and empathise. People feel good reading books that suggest there is a new easy shortcut to success – whether it is reducing a waistline or increasing a bottom line. Even when there's no shortcut, it's human nature to be drawn to success stories. They are entertaining, uplifting and inspiring. But there's a key difference between being appealing and being useful.

Which brings me to my second problem with these books. It's not just that there are so many of them – it's that so many of them are rubbish and have obviously been written for the enrichment of the author, not the reader.

It's my belief that, far from providing the answers, reading too many business books distracts people from the real issues, misleading them into thinking there's a magic formula they can transfer from other companies, and generally making them feel inadequate.

As I look back over my career it's overwhelmingly clear to me that the best lessons on how to succeed in business rarely come from either business itself or business books, but from life experiences. This makes it even more of a shame that half the business people I know don't *have* a life. Many senior executives spend over two-thirds of their waking hours in an office only ever talking to other executives. It's just not real life. It's execulife.

If you spend the bulk of your time in the business lounges of airports or staring at the computer on your desk you can come to forget that business is *a part of life*. Your frame of reference becomes narrower and narrower until all you care about is your competitors and the financial analysts.

I know senior fast-food executives who believe they can only really learn from other fast-food businesses and executives. I know senior car manufacturers who believe they can only learn lessons from the car industry. Yet the plain fact is that whatever business you happen to be in you have to work with other people. They are your workforce and your consumers. And it's with them that the real lessons lie. People are driven by things like love, hate, jealousy, self-interest, fear, ambition. Most people share a craving to belong and a desperate desire to be appreciated. If you take this view, the canvas for business learning explodes. You no longer have to just look at your industry sector, or industry in general, for lessons on how to get the best out of the people you work with.

I was reminded of this a couple of months into my third break on a windy Sunday morning at the end of the junior soccer season. My twins' team, the Dragons, had somehow got into the semi-final of their under-10 league. I say 'somehow' because Errol (the coach) and I (the assistant coach) had a somewhat, er, relaxed attitude towards training. Forget winning at all costs – this team was to be about fun and fitness and friendship. So while other teams had a training session mid-week, we preferred simply to get the girls to turn up a bit early before each match so we could have a kick around.

It was more about character building than winning trophies. Which was just as well, really, since we didn't stand a prayer of winning any trophies.

The team we were playing on this particular Sunday was Coogee United and they were hot favourites to win the final, having beaten all before them, including us 3–0 the last time we'd played them. This semi-final would be little more than a formality.

As usual, by the time our players started to arrive in dribs and drabs the entire Coogee United team were already in their kit and well into some serious drills. To make matters worse, as kickoff got nearer and nearer it became clear we wouldn't even have a full team. You're supposed to have nine players, but by the time the ref called us onto the pitch we only had seven. No worries, I thought; Coogee had a full team as well as three subs.

I walked over and introduced myself to the Coogee United coach, then said, 'Sorry about this, but a number of our girls have called in sick so we've only got seven today. Any chance you could lend us one of your subs and we make it eight a side for this game?' I asked him.

'No,' he said.

'Excuse me?' I said, slightly stunned.

'Listen, mate, it's the semi-final. It's not my fault if you can't field a full team.'

'Oh, fair enough, we'll play with seven then,' I said.

Looking around at the huge pitch as I walked back to talk to Errol, I couldn't help thinking that with one of the girls in goal the other six would hardly be able to see each other let alone pass to each other. It wasn't looking good. I desperately didn't want the girls to end the season feeling humiliated or demoralised. Call me an idealist, but I thought the idea behind kids' sports was to give them a lifelong love of the game, not put them off forever.

Given our previous 3–0 loss to Coogee, with two fewer players I didn't dare imagine what the score might end up being. Less than sixty seconds after kickoff we were already one down. Three minutes later it was 2–0.

Fearing the worst, Errol and I strode the touchline calling out encouragement.

And then something magical started to happen.

Our goalie made a great save. Then another. And another. One of our midfielders lost the ball in a tackle and then actually won it back off the opponent who had taken it from her. Our left back went for a searing run down the wing, holding off numerous challenges. Five minutes went by and the Dragons still hadn't conceded another goal, and as halftime approached it was *still* 2–0. The parents on the sideline joined in with the encouragement. 'Great save, Leah!' 'Excellent defence, Grace!' 'Wonderful pass, Ilana!' 'Come on, Dragons!'

We spent the last ten minutes of the first half desperately defending our goal and somehow managed to stop the ball crossing our line. Finally the halftime whistle went and the girls gathered in a tight circle for their oranges and the team talk. They all looked shattered, having run themselves ragged due to their lack of numbers. Despite their heroic first half I knew once they ran out of puff the goals would start flowing again for Coogee. Nevertheless it had been an incredible performance and I urged them to give it their best shot in the second half despite the odds.

'Amazing stuff, girls. Simply amazing. I've never been prouder. Taylor – fabulous. Evie, best half I've seen you play. Manon and Isabella, you're playing out of your skin. All of you – wonderful. You've completely surprised them. They thought you'd be easy beats but you're doing brilliantly. Let's raise it up a notch in the second half and really show them what the Dragons are made of. Drink lots of water because you've got a lot of running to do. Get your breath back and then give it everything over the next thirty minutes as this is the last game we'll play for a while.'

'Unless we get to the final,' Isabella corrected me as she reached for another orange segment.

Fuck me. There I am secretly hoping to keep the score line respectable and she's thinking they can win! All the girls certainly looked determined. There was no messing about like there usually was at halftime. They appeared focused and eager – egging each other on and making suggestions as they drank from their water bottles. As they ran out for the second half in their ill-fitting shirts and mismatched socks to face off against their immaculately uniformed opposition, I had a lump in my throat. God, I loved them.

As we waited for the whistle I found myself willing them on like no other team before. The opening passages of play weren't exactly promising as again our line was constantly besieged by the bigger, more numerous and better drilled opposition. But still they held out.

The Dragons were all red in the face and panting, but they simply refused to ease up – in fact, it seemed as if they were playing with more intensity as the match wore on. The atmosphere was incredible. Fifteen minutes into the second half it was *still* 2–0, and most of the play was now happening in the opposition's half.

I don't know what came over me but I heard myself yelling, 'Come on, Dragons, ten minutes and only two goals needed.' And here's the thing – it didn't sound ridiculous.

It was seven on nine, yet we were more than holding our own. The other team actually looked rattled as they fell back to defend their goal. The last five minutes was as exciting a sporting spectacle as I've ever seen (and I've been to *a lot* of international sport). The Dragons were simply inspired – playing for each other, believing in themselves, and ignoring the odds.

It was uplifting, moving and somehow important to witness.

When the final whistle went it was still 2–0. The crowd burst into raucous applause. The Coogee team, coach and parents were generous in their congratulations (they did indeed go on to win the final afterwards). The tournament organiser made a special announcement about the Dragons' heroic performance over the tannoy and the cheers got even wilder. It was a genuinely joyous scene.

Yet we had lost the game.

And it was only an under-10s girls' soccer game at that.

I won't patronise you with all the obvious lessons beyond saying there was more to be learnt about how to create business success from that match than there was from all the business books I have read put together.

The Magnificent Seven

19

Abbeyview

The night of the Dragons game I called my father to tell him all about it. Though it'd been over seven years since we moved Dad into his nursing home, I still found making telephone calls to him almost as upsetting as visiting.

It's quite difficult to talk to someone on the phone if there's no response. At least if you're with the person you can look them in the eye or hold their hand. On the phone it's just silence. Many times I've wondered whether Dad even knows it's me who's talking to him. However, I keep calling in the hope that it might give him some small flash of happiness or pleasure. Whether it does or not is impossible to tell. Still, given I'm halfway around the world and can't visit him more than once or twice a year, I like to call him every week – however hard I might find it.

Over the years I've developed a routine to make the calls easier. First off I write down a long list of all the things I want to say. This may sound rather planned and unnatural, but when you're talking into a silent phone it helps. In the early years I tried a few spontaneous off-the-cuff conversations but they were a disaster. No matter how hard I tried, if I hadn't done at least some preparation I would inevitably end up mumbling then quickly falling silent myself.

The second part of the routine is that I call the nursing home in advance to check that it's a good time and so they can take a cordless phone to his room. I'd quickly learnt that if Dad was having a meal or being bathed, a call from a weepy son in Australia was a pain in the arse that everyone could well do without.

Third, I take the dog out for a long walk while making the call. This last point is very important as I find having our 'conversations' overheard by other people – even my own family – awkward and upsetting.

Finally, I have trained myself to leave huge pauses between every sentence. It sounds moronic if you hear me doing it.

'Hi, Dad, it's your younger son Nigel calling from Australia.'

Then I say nothing for a full seven seconds.

'The kids and Kate are well.'

1 . . . 2 . . . 3 . . . 4 . . . 5 . . . 6 . . . 7 . . .

'They all send their love.'

1 . . . 2 . . . 3 . . . 4 . . . 5 . . . 6 . . . 7 . . .

And so on.

The reason I do this is I have been told that when people are talking to sufferers of dementia and Parkinson's they often don't give the patient time to form and speak a thought. They may have heard you and want to say something, but if you've steamrollered on at normal pace the moment is lost, and in many cases that might be the only thing they say to you in an entire year. So, cue the long pauses.

I didn't hold out much hope for any response on this occasion as Dad hadn't said anything to me for months, so it was lovely when I called back and the nurse who answered the phone greeted me with the words: 'Hi, it's Nigel, isn't it? I'll put you on to your dad – his face lit up when I told him his son was going to call from Australia. John? John. Wake up, John. It's Nigel, your son.'

'Hi, Dad. It's your son, Nigel, calling from Australia.'

1 . . . 2 . . . 3 . . . 4 . . . 5 . . . 6 . . . 7 . . .

'Love you very much. All's fine here.'

1 . . . 2 . . . 3 . . . 4 . . . 5 . . . 6 . . . 7 . . .

And so on, to total silence, for five minutes.

I told him about the Dragons' victory; the amazing things Harry was bringing home from his carpentry lessons at school; Alex's refereeing progress; Kate's job offer and potential return to the workforce. I didn't tell him that I'd left my job as the first time I'd taken a corporate break it had made him awfully anxious. Instead I blithely made up a pack of lies about how well I was doing at the office.

I don't just lie in these conversations – I lie afterwards when I go home, telling all the kids how pleased Granfie was to hear of their news and how he'd sent them all his love. I just can't face telling them I have no idea whether Granfie understood a word I'd said and that he'd said nothing whatsoever in return.

A nurse has to hold the phone for Dad so I'm aware that I'm always talking to two people rather than just Dad. Much as I hate having our intimacy and misery listened to, it does sometimes have its advantages. For example, during this call, I was interrupted by his carer.

'Nigel, it's Sue here, sorry to interrupt but I could hear you were ending up and I just wanted to say your father is trying to say something,' the nurse said.

'Oh – thank you,' I replied.

I had got to the end of my list so was momentarily lost for words. I listened intently. Dad's breathing was getting heavy and it sounded like he was trying to speak.

'Dad, I know it's hard to talk, there's no need to rush.'

1 . . . 2 . . . 3 . . . 4 . . . 5 . . . 6 . . . 7 . . .

'It's night-time in Australia and I'm taking the dog for a walk.'

1 . . . 2 . . . 3 . . . 4 . . . 5 . . . 6 . . . 7 . . .

'Come on, John – louder,' Sue said firmly.

1 . . . 2 . . . 3 . . . 4 . . . 5 . . . 6 . . . 7 . . .

'He's mouthing something. Come on, John, louder now. You can do it. Concentrate.'

1 . . . 2 . . . 3 . . . 4 . . . 5 . . . 6 . . . 7 . . .

'No worries, Dad. Don't stress. We love you very much. I'll call next week.'

I was about to hang up when Sue said, 'No! Hold on, Nigel. Sorry to bark at you – but he *is* going to say something. He just needs a little bit more time.'

1 . . . 2 . . . 3 . . . 4 . . . 5 . . . 6 . . . 7 . . .

'Ner . . .' he whispered.

'Yes, Dad?'

'Ner . . .' he whispered again, a bit louder this time. 'Ner . . . Nigel – God bless you,' he said as clear as a bell.

I'd like to tell you we then had a long, loving conversation, but the sad reality is that he immediately fell silent. Indeed, at the time of writing he hasn't spoken a word to me since.

I took the dog on a particularly long walk that night; I dragged the poor thing around the streets for over an hour. When I eventually got back home I was too upset to indulge in my normal 'Granfie was fascinated by your news' routine.

'How was Granfie, Daddy?' Grace asked.

Now it was my turn to be silent.

'Have you been crying, Daddy?' Eve asked.

Silence.

'Did you tell him about our game today?' Grace said.

I stifled a sob.

'Leave Daddy, girls, he needs to go to his room,' Kate said as she gently ushered me upstairs out of everyone's way.

20

From Obelisk to Cobblers

There's one thing that always makes me feel better no matter what my emotional state: a swim in the ocean.

It never fails to clear my head, give me a better perspective on life and remind me to count my blessings. I can see why the locals refer to our local beach as Dr Bronte. I find even the briefest of dips in this particularly beautiful part of the world reinvigorating.

Only one thing is better than a swim in the ocean and that's a *nude* swim in the ocean. A bit like my numbers obsession it's not something I've ever really been comfortable shouting about, but I'm yet to come across the bad mood a skinny-dip in the sea can't transform into joy.

Leaving aside for the moment that it feels absolutely fabulous while you're doing it, I invariably come out of the sea feeling somehow reborn. I don't want to get all religious on you, but it has a redemptive, baptismal vibe to it. Which is why, every now and then, I sneak off to one or another of Sydney's nudist beaches for a swim. After the God-bless-you call with my dad I felt another nude ocean swim was in order. Given that the next day I was giving a speech in the beautiful harbourside suburb of Mosman, I decided I would pack my running kit, goggles and a towel (no swimmers, obviously, as I wouldn't be needing them) so I could go for a run and skinny-dip before I headed home.

I love discovering new parts of Sydney and constantly scour the map for new places to run or swim. My study of the map on this occasion revealed that on my way home I would be a short detour away from Middle Head, which was an area of the harbour I had never previously visited. And not only was Middle Harbour a national park perfect for running in, it also had not one but two nudist beaches. Cobblers Beach was on the north side of the head and Obelisk Beach was on the south side. Gotta love Sydney.

I resolved that after my speech I'd drive to Middle Head, go for a run ending up at Cobblers Beach, throw my clothes off and dive into the harbour.

The speech went well and the weather was perfect as I parked in Middle Head. It was one of those heavenly winter days in Sydney where the sky is bright blue and there isn't a wisp of cloud to be seen. Just warm sunshine and a gentle breeze. I took one last look at the map to remind myself of my route and set off. I felt slightly euphoric as I jogged along at an easy pace with just my thoughts and the beautiful scenery to occupy me. Half an hour later, I got to the top of the path to Cobblers Beach and sped up, eager to burst onto the beach and jump in the water.

I did indeed burst onto the beach, but I didn't jump in the water. Instead I gave a rather pathetic yelp, turned on my heels and ran back up the path. I'd been so lost in visions of a totally deserted, secluded, unspoilt strip of sand that it hadn't occurred to me that there might be anyone else on the beach in the middle of a working day in mid-winter. How many other people would have the freedom, or indeed inclination, to sit naked on a beach at such a time? Quite a few people, apparently, as ten or so heads (attached to ten or so naked male bodies) had turned and gazed at me rather disdainfully as I hit the sand.

I was disappointed, but was still determined to go for a naked swim. I'd just have to go to Obelisk instead.

As I ran down the path to Obelisk Beach I was more cautious than before, listening intently and peering around corners for other people. This time my vision was accurate. Not only was Obelisk deserted it was also secluded, beautiful, unspoilt – everything I'd imagined. I stripped off my kit and dived into the water. Jesus wept, it was cold, but all the more exhilarating for it. I couldn't help letting out one of those annoying American whoops. Then a 'Yeah!'

After a few brief minutes' swimming I walked up onto the sand rubbing my head with the salt water (since giving up shampoo it's as good a wash as my hair ever gets). I was still standing naked on the beach as the Sydney to Manly passenger ferry came into view and slowly steamed past on its way to Circular Quay. I don't know what came over me but, rather than rush for my towel, I raised my arms to the heavens and waved my hands while shouting 'Woohooo!' A few startled passengers pointed and waved back from the deck. I ran back into the water laughing my arse off. I like to think my father would have approved.

Later, when I was driving home, I was suddenly struck by a thought.

I had run from Cobblers Beach to Obelisk Beach – wouldn't it be inexpressibly more fabulous to swim from one to the other instead? Not only that, wouldn't it be laugh-out-loud, hug-your-sides, praise-the-stars fantastic to do it naked? Moreover, wasn't it about time I got over myself and conquered my fear of swimming naked when there was another human on the beach? Why not do this swim as a race with lots of other people? A sort of Bondi to Bronte without the clothes.

Just like when you sing at weddings it's not much fun if no one else does but it's simply amazing when the whole congregation joins in, wouldn't doing a mass skinny dip simply multiply the joy you feel when you go for one alone? Wouldn't it be the most uplifting, hilarious, cleansing, pure, grounding event ever?

Every year we could do some good by raising money for the national park and raising awareness of environmental issues, while having a boatload of fun. The location was perfect. And the distance of about one and a half kilometres was just right. Surely regulations wouldn't be a problem as they were both nudist beaches anyway. It would be a way to throw off the straitjacket of modern over-commercialised life, get back to basics, remind people of the simple things and what's really important in life. A chance to be utterly authentic and stick two fingers up at all those ludicrous, airbrushed images of bodily perfection in the magazines.

It would also be a safe opportunity to rebel and be ever-so-slightly naughty. I mean, you'd be naked, but it's not like anyone else would be able to see you – you'd be in the water the whole time. Why couldn't Sydney have another famous iconic communal event on its calendar? Every year I do the barefoot classic on Bondi Beach and love it for its unique Australian vibe – what's not to like about running barefoot on one of the world's most famous beaches with a bunch of other happy people? If that's fun, just imagine how joyous an experience a bare-butt communal swim in the world's most beautiful harbour would be.

The more I thought about it the more I liked the idea. As a first step I registered the name The Sydney Skinny and then purchased the domain for good measure.

Conversations with the relevant harbour authority and an events company who regularly put on other world-class events went so well that if I can get a founding sponsor prepared to stump up a few grand in advance we'd be good to go. Admittedly clothing branding opportunities would be limited as there wouldn't *be* any clothing. But, mildly deluded or not, I'm hoping the potential to hand out, say, 'Just Done It' Nike towels or 'Nothing added natural juice' Nudie bottles to competitors as they come out of the water at the finishing line is too good an opportunity to be passed up. I can be contacted via my website . . .

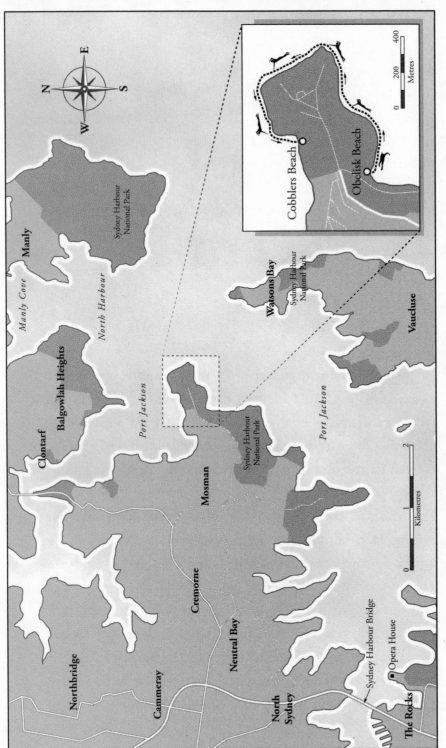

The Obelisk to Cobblers Sydney Skinny route

21

The Letter

As the three-month anniversary of leaving the office approached I was generally satisfied with the progress I was making. Admittedly I was still only taking baby steps, but I was cooking, exercising, losing weight, reading more of the books I actually wanted to read and spending substantial time with the family. After repeated pestering I had just restarted the 'Dad's Trips' I'd instituted last time I took a career break. This involved taking each of the kids out by themselves. We didn't go anywhere fancy; the trips were designed so I could spend some one-on-one time with them.

I was even chillaxed about our money situation, with more speaking engagements than I could have ever dreamt of booked over the coming months. And though the money I made at speaking gigs wouldn't add up to what my job had paid me previously, it would mean we'd be able to get by. I'm a big believer in the 'philosophy of enough'. If you have a clear understanding of your personal 'enough' points in each area of your life it can be enormously liberating and engender a deep sea of calm and happiness. The macho philosophy that 'good enough isn't enough' is hugely damaging and makes thousands of people miserable as they agonise about the next step up, when in reality they would be far better served to develop a sense of gratitude for what they currently have. So while we were having to tighten our belts, I didn't find it an unpleasant experience; to my mind we were extremely fortunate to have enough in most areas.

But *my* feelings were only one side of the equation. Kate had her own views and they weren't quite as 'head in the clouds, everything in the garden is rosy' as mine. For a start, she felt pressured to go back to work. Irrespective of how many times I told her to only return to the workforce if she wanted to, she simply couldn't shake the notion that if I wasn't going to work she had to. And, understandably, she didn't want to be pushed back to work by me. It was as if I had broken an unwritten contract that stated we would forever divide the labour along the same lines. It felt to her that by staying home I was in some way stealing *her* job – literally making her redundant. But she didn't want to be laid off and she was scared I wouldn't do as good a job as she herself did.

She also felt vulnerable. It's a huge thing for a woman to give up her career and put her entire financial security and future in the hands of her partner. It takes an enormous amount of trust, but she'd done it. And now here I was, giving up regular employment again. As confident as I was that we would all be fine – more than fine – I understood her feelings. 'Resentment' might be overstating her position, but 'fear' wouldn't be entirely inaccurate.

It was at the height of this fear that The Letter arrived.

Every year I receive a letter from the financial institution that looks after my modest investment account in the UK. I started it during the early years of my career, when financial advisers were adamant that every home-owning couple in the UK should have a thing called an Endowment. The idea was simple: you agreed to give a regular sum to a financial institution every month and commit to not touching it for twenty-five years; they'd invest the money for you and, come your fifties, you'd get a lump sum to pay off your mortgage. These so-called endowment-linked mortgages soon became the most popular type of home loan. Banks would give you an interest-only loan for the principal sum on your house if you had an endowment that was projected to pay out the capital amount of the loan in twenty-five years' time. The financial projections for endowment-linked mortgages weren't given by some shonky fly-by-night salesmen either; they were made and verified by all the major respected financial institutions in the UK. They'd show you graphs of what your money would be worth in twenty-five years if it grew by nine per cent or fourteen per cent. All very reassuring and rather exciting. Many of my friends took out huge endowments, basically betting their whole financial security on them. Although sceptical, I decided to take one out, however I refused to link it to my mortgage or to invest a large amount per month, instead settling on a very modest sum.

'It's hardly worth the bother, Nigel – you'll regret this later, I guarantee,' my financial adviser remarked at the time.

But I remained adamant. I just didn't want to commit myself to a regular payment I couldn't get out of – and one of the things that was kept quiet, if not hidden, was that you *couldn't* get out of it. If you stopped paying your monthly sums at any time during the twenty-five-year period you were penalised so eye-wateringly by your financial provider that you were essentially locked in for the whole term. I also felt a deep-seated distrust of the promises made about the future returns – for which I was roundly ridiculed at the time.

'You'll never get anywhere playing it so safe, Nigel,' I was told a hundred times. 'Besides, the returns are as good as guaranteed.'

All well and good if the projections were guaranteed. Or even half accurate.

Turns out they were neither.

All it took was for the markets to hit a rocky patch and many of the funds went down, not up. Mine, which was hilariously called a 'managed growth' fund, was among the ones that went down, even though I had gone for the most conservative product on offer.

As you'd expect, there was a huge fuss. People were appalled to discover that they were linked into decades-long savings schemes that would produce nothing remotely close to what they'd been led to believe. Many faced financial ruin as the recalculated projections of the final endowment payouts revealed their sum wouldn't come close to paying back their mortgage – *which was the entire reason they had taken them out in the first place.*

In response to this scandal the British government, to its credit, introduced tough new rules on what financial advisers and institutions could say about projected returns for such funds. And how they could say it. Henceforth they had to emphasise to prospective customers that there were no certainties and to stress that past performance was no guarantee of future returns. They also had to write to all their existing customers and come clean with them regarding what their investment was really likely to deliver. Something along the lines of: 'Contrary to what we promised when we were selling the investment, it is now only worth half of what we projected.' Embarrassing at the best of times, I'm sure. But what my institution, along with countless others, actually said was quite different.

Dear Mr Marsh,

RED ALERT: HIGH RISK OF A SHORTFALL

We believe there is a high risk that your plan will not pay out enough to cover the target amount when it matures. We strongly suggest you consider taking action if you have not already done so.

They then detail the likely amount of the shortfall and list some of the options available to me to avert total financial catastrophe. I hardly need add that none of these options involve the company making good on its previous predictions . . .

The Letter is just wrong on so many levels.

Where's the apology? Why no empathy? Yet they send it every year. I suggest an improvement would be something along the lines of:

Dear Mr Marsh,

We are devastated to realise that we talked you and countless others like you into a significant twenty-five-year commit-ment under false premises. Not only did we overstate the likely financial returns of our product, we also dramatically exaggerated our expertise and competence. Although we didn't intend to ruin your life we understand that you, rightly, will never trust us again. We can understand the hatred you must feel towards us knowing that we got paid, and continue to charge you, for this product irrespective of the woefully inadequate returns.

Contrary to all the bollocks we consistently talk about the stock market *always* outperforming ordinary savings accounts we acknowledge that this is a self-serving lie and, indeed, you would have been far better off putting your cash under your mattress than paying us huge fees to make your money worth substantially less than the amount you gave us in the first place. Like many of the others we have betrayed you may be facing a catastrophic inability to pay off your mortgage when we make your final payment so we seriously urge you to take financial advice from someone more trustworthy and competent than us about how to address this shortfall.

Unfortunately, the brutal financial reality of running a large publicly quoted firm means we can't offer you a refund or stop charging you a monthly fee, and we are embarrassed to admit we will be continuing to make a profit out of shrinking your savings for you. For all of the above reasons, we obviously don't expect you to accept our deepest apologies but we sincerely extend them all the same.

Humbly yours,

Big Bank

Now that's a financial institution I'd have some time for.

22

Yvonne Fletcher

To be fair to the bank that sends me The Letter, I am a bit of a harsh judge. I've long been fascinated by people's ethics. How they behave individually and collectively – whether it's as a company or as a government. Ethics was one of the subjects I majored in at university all those years ago as a young theology student. My decision to study ethics was confirmed by two events in London during the 1980s – the first in 1980, the second in 1984.

In 1980 I was a callow sixteen-year-old at boarding school in Oxfordshire when the news broke that a group of armed Iranian Arab separatists had taken over the Iranian embassy in central London and were holding over twenty hostages at gunpoint. This was *huge* news. Not only was it happening barely thirty miles away, but it was happening slap-bang in the middle of England's capital city. It was headline news around the world and at school it became the *only* topic of conversation.

The terrorists wanted autonomy for Iran's Khuzestan Province and were insisting on the release of Arab prisoners held in Khuzestan's jails. Irrespective of the merits of this cause, their demand did reveal they had rather a loose grip on reality when it came to the British government's sphere of control. The government did the best they could in impossible circumstances. The safety of the hostages and the general public at large was the key concern. Professional negotiators were brought in; food, drink and telecommunications were supplied to the terrorists; respectful discussions urged a peaceful conclusion. As negotiations continued over the ensuing days, however, the terrorists became increasingly strident and threatening until on day six they announced that unless their demands were met immediately they would start shooting a hostage at regular intervals until they got what they wanted. The drama, tension and suspense were more intense than anything Hollywood could dream up. And this was real, not some Bruce Willis movie. To a sixteen-year-old schoolboy with a keen sense of right and wrong it was all-consuming. What the hell was going to happen?

On the sixth day of the siege I walked from my school to the local chip shop to buy my regular revoltingly unhealthy dinner of curry sauce and chips. As with every other shop, restaurant and pub in the country at the time, live coverage of the siege was showing on the TV behind the counter. As I queued to place my order the terrorists shot one of their hostages in cold blood and rolled his dead body down the embassy steps. I stared at the screen in stunned disbelief. I still remember the burning anger I felt and thinking, 'You murderous fuckers, you don't get away with that shit in Britain.'

As if in answer to my thoughts, just twenty-three minutes later soldiers from the SAS stormed the embassy. I watched the whole thing from start to finish on live TV in a high street chip shop with six strangers who were similarly transfixed. The SAS – dressed from head to toe in black – abseiled down the building on ropes and swung through the embassy's windows, throwing smoke bombs and shooting as they proceeded. They killed five out of the six terrorists and freed the hostages. Unfortunately, one of the terrorists murdered another of the hostages before the rescue was complete but, despite this tragedy, by any measure it was a resounding victory for right. Real boys' own stuff. To my young self it was proof positive that although there might be evil people in this world and nasty shit does unfortunately happen, the arc of justice is long and the good guys win in the end. The only surviving terrorist was tried and sentenced to life imprisonment.

The idea that good eventually triumphs over evil remained my broad world view until four years later, when the comfortable moral fabric of my universe was irretrievably shaken and rearranged. Again, the location was a central London embassy – this time the Libyan one. A group of Libyan dissidents had informed the police they were going to protest outside the Libyan embassy. The police sent a number of officers to ensure everything remained peaceful and to protect the embassy and its staff. During the demonstration a member of the Libyan embassy staff (or the 'Libyan People's Bureau' as they then liked to be called) leant out of the window and sprayed the crowd and police with automatic gunfire.

A number of people were hit, including a young female police officer called Yvonne Fletcher, who was shot in the back by the very people she was protecting. She was unarmed, engaged to be married, twenty-five years old. And dead.

I remember weeping at the news reports – and feeling the same sense of righteous anger that I had felt four years before in the chip shop watching the body of that hostage roll down the steps. But this time I waited in vain for the avenging angels on ropes because – and I find it hard not to quiver with fury as I type this – we didn't ensure right prevailed. Instead, *we provided the murderer with a police escort out of the country because he had diplomatic immunity.*

That was twenty-eight years ago and ever since I have been fascinated by how people decide to act – and how they explain those actions to themselves and others. Hearing an ex-editor of the *News of the World* openly admit that he hacked an actor's emails and mobile phone 'because he was rich', as if that somehow justified criminal behaviour, is but one recent example. Leaving tough decisions to the 'experts' just isn't enough (as the UK government's actions after Yvonne Fletcher's cold-blooded murder starkly made clear to me). I can't think of a more important topic to be taught in our schools than ethics and I was overjoyed to learn that my sons' school does just that – they are studying the topic just as I did at university.

That's not to say I agree with all their conclusions when they come home, but at least it forces them to *think* about their actions. In an increasingly secular world I suspect the next generation is going to need this capacity more than ever.

23

Lampshade

Being interested in ethics in no way means I can claim the moral high ground regarding my own actions. Indeed I'm constantly stunned by how people, usually whipped up by the popular media, can demonise others when they fall short and make mistakes. Each of us is fallible, after all. For example, when I read the newspaper reports of some unfortunate mother who has lost a child because she neglected to hold their hand when they were standing by a road or took her eye off them when they were at the beach, I don't think – as sections of our society clearly do – 'Silly cow, let's publicly castigate her in her hour of abject misery.' I think, 'Poor woman. There but for the grace of God go I.'

Recently my dear friend and weight-loss teammate Thomas confided that the week before she had fed her baby daughter a teaspoon of *flea poison* rather than flu medicine in the middle of the night. And, worse, she hadn't realised her mistake until the next morning when she opened the fridge and screamed in horror upon seeing the bottles side by side on the same shelf.

I felt her horror particularly keenly because of an incident that took place ten years ago and still wakes me up at night in a cold sweat. We were on holiday in the UK and had met up with a group of friends for New Year's Eve. We had all kept in touch since we'd met at college and often went away together during the festive season. At first it was just couples, but as we all had kids the group became pretty big. It was nigh on impossible to rent a house large enough for all of us so we'd begun to rent cottages that were next door to each other. This meant each family could retire to their own domain during the hideous bedtime hours, but when all the kids were asleep the adults could reconvene in one of the cottages for the evening's festivities. It was an easy matter to nip back and check on the kids and on this particular holiday the baby monitors worked between the different cottages so there was no pressing need to do even that.

It's hard to look back on my actions on the night in question as in retrospect they seem so moronic and lethally irresponsible. The shame and guilt I feel is only matched by the relief that a tragedy was averted, though at the time I thought I was being considerate and loving. We were all meeting for dinner in the next-door cottage and Kate had left me to settle the kids before joining the group.

All four of our kids were sleeping in the same room. I finished their bedtime story and made sure all the windows were closed as it was snowing outside and the cottage, which had no central heating, was freezing. As I turned the light out our younger lad, Harry, asked if I could leave it on. When I turned it back on his elder brother complained he wouldn't be able to get to sleep because it was too bright. I then spent ten minutes trying different combinations of hall light on/room light off, bathroom light on/hall light off to get to a degree of light that was acceptable to all. Nothing I came up with seemed to satisfy everyone. Until, that is, I struck on a brilliant idea. I turned all the lights off bar the bedside lamp – *which I put a pillow over to dim the light.* All the kids agreed the gentle warm glow was perfect, so after checking with Kate that the baby monitor was working next door I gave each of the kids a final goodnight kiss and went to join the adults.

Dinner was being served when I arrived. The baby monitors were silent, everyone was relaxed and happy, the wine flowed. This was back in the day when I both drank and smoked. I not only smoked between courses, but during them. We all did. On this evening the group managed to smoke so many cigarettes that we ran out before the second course.

'Nigel, there's a fresh pack in my handbag in our kitchen,' Kate said.

'No worries, I'll just be a second,' I replied as I got up from the table to go next door to our cottage.

Sure enough, there was an unopened pack of Marlboros in Kate's handbag just inside the front door. While I was there I thought I'd quickly pop my head into the kids' room to check all was well. As I pushed the door open I was met with an unmistakeably acrid smell. There were gentle wisps of smoke coming from the pillow on the lamp.

I ran over and ripped it off the lampshade. To my horror, the entire underside of the pillow was singed black. Close up, the toxic smell from the cheap foam material inside was sickening. The kids were still fast asleep and blissfully unaware. I opened their windows and went and sat on the kitchen floor.

I was as white as a sheet and shaking. I felt physically sick. Not from the smell but from the realisation that I had almost just killed all my children. If I hadn't come back at that moment we would have returned to that room to find four corpses. At least a fire would have been noticeable – but smoke inhalation is a silent killer.

I felt self-hatred on a level previously unimaginable. How was it possible to be so stupid? What on earth had I been thinking? Did I even have a brain? I'd been a total inexcusable idiot. Forget what I felt – what would I ever have said to my wife? To my family? To the police?

'Yes, Kate, I put them to bed and then put a flammable toxic pillow above a hot light bulb. Yes, and I shut all the windows as well. Then I went next door while they asphyxiated to death.'

The horror as I relive the consequences that could have occurred if we hadn't run out of cigarettes that evening is every bit as awful today as it was that night. And imagine how it would have been reported once the facts of the tragedy were revealed.

No, on sober reflection – ethics studies or not – I don't think I've *ever* got the right to judge others in their hour of personal failure. The fact is shit happens – whether due to parental idiocy or just random unavoidable bad luck – and when it does, we'd all do well to look inside ourselves for an empathetic and supportive response, not a censorious and judgemental one.

24

Pretty Woman

To date I might have been fortunate enough to have avoided accidentally harming any of my kids but, thrilled as we were with this state of affairs, over the years Kate had become just as worried about accidentally *having* more kids as damaging the ones we'd already got. She had good cause for concern as by a biological quirk of fate we seemed to be one of the more fertile couples on earth. Early in our marriage I convinced her to come off the pill, arguing that in a few years' time we'd want to start a family and it could take us some time to conceive.

Yep – pregnant four weeks later.

When we were ready to think about number two she stopped taking the pill and, contrary to the belief that lightning doesn't strike in the same place twice, four weeks later we discovered she was pregnant again.

From then on it was full-body condoms, the pill and the rhythm method every time we had sex. Until, that is, we had an extra bottle of wine in Paris and I must have winked at her – because, you've guessed it, four weeks later we learnt she was pregnant yet again. This time with twins.

So there was ample evidence that we had to be careful. To start with, Kate had been the one to take responsibility for contraception. Not for any unfair gender reasons, but because in so many ways the pill just happens to be the best, most convenient method of birth control. People talk a lot of rubbish about how inequitable it is that in relationships more women are on the pill than men use condoms, but it is a ridiculous comparison to make. If there was a properly developed, fully approved and commonly available male pill it would be right to criticise men for not taking it in equal numbers, but the female equivalent of the male condom isn't taking the pill – the female equivalent of the male condom is the female condom. And how well has that caught on? Precisely.

However, it is a big ask to expect a woman to put all those chemicals in her body for whole decades at a time. It was entirely understandable, therefore, that as the years wore on Kate suggested it might just be time for me to take a turn. Which is all well and good, but I have a passionate aversion to condoms. I mean, come on, no one seriously believes all that advertising bollocks about them being 'fun to put on and barely there feather-light', do they? In terms of great inventions they're right up there with cigarettes and leg warmers if you ask me. There are two types of men – those who admit condoms are awful passion-killing disasters, and liars.

And so the V word was raised.

Now I'm naturally squeamish at the best of times, but the thought of having someone operate on my old fella makes me ill. But a vasectomy had been raised and so a vasectomy was officially and unavoidably on the agenda. Logically I knew I didn't have even a hint of a leg to stand on. But for men (or this man anyway), logic only gets you so far when you're talking about your crown jewels. Especially with the plethora of horror stories doing the rounds. Over the years people have told me about blokes with permanently bent erections, blokes who couldn't *get* erections, blokes with painful purple balls, blokes with swollen balls the size of melons, blokes who lost their sex drive and, most distressingly, blokes who had got their wives pregnant after the operation anyway. It was hardly encouraging for a fully signed up genital coward such as myself.

Beyond these gory examples of what could go wrong there was a more subconscious resistance I'm slightly embarrassed about. Although I might be as far away from being an alpha male as possible without actually wearing a dress, deep down I couldn't quite rid myself of the thought that if I was firing blanks I would somehow be 'less of a man'. As I said, I'm not particularly proud of this thinking, but I suspect many men secretly feel the same. You can come off the pill; you can't come off the vasectomy.

In the end it was a mate visiting from overseas who got me over the line. 'Nige,' he said, 'it's the gentlemanly thing to do.' I don't know why that phrase struck home so much, but I signed up the next day. The operation itself wasn't a drama as – much to the horror of my brother, who had had his done years earlier – I ticked the 'I'm a big girl's blouse and want a general anaesthetic' box so I didn't feel a thing. Jonathon had his done with a local anaesthetic, chatted cheerfully to the doctor through the procedure, and was at work by ten the same morning. I, on the other hand, went home and spent the rest of the day in bed. It's pretty clear it was the right Marsh brother who joined the army.

However it wasn't any physical aftereffects that left an impression on me; it was the conversation I had with a friend the next week. This particular friend, like me, was reluctant to have a vasectomy. Unlike me, he refused to be swayed.

When I pressed him for the real reason behind his intransigence he said, 'You've got to bear in mind, Nigel, it's a permanent step. Women can't have babies after a certain time anyway, but men can father children well into old age. Charlie Chaplin had a kid in his mid-seventies. I'll never have a vasectomy because if I get married again my new wife might want kids.'

'But you're already married!' I spluttered.

'Yeah, I know, and I'm happy – but never say never. No one knows what the future holds.'

I couldn't help but be shocked by his attitude. I don't want to be sanctimonious, tempt fate or take anything for granted, but my intention is to be married forever. To the same person. Whether I am or not is another matter, but that is at least what

I *plan* around. To my mind, if you plan for the possibility that you might get divorced it simply increases the chance that you *will* get divorced.

Clearly, however, I'm hugely out of step with the times. Recently I went onto the *Huffington Post* website and was surprised to see that alongside the 'Sport' and 'Arts' and 'Politics' sections they also had a 'Divorce' one. Intrigued, I clicked on the tab and spent a horrified afternoon reading article upon article by intelligent articulate women celebrating the joys of divorce. Now let's be very clear: I don't think people should be forced to stay married – and divorce in many circumstances is obviously the best option – but some of these articles were taking the piss. In their own way these women were little better than that Kardashian woman who was married for seventy-two minutes or whatever it was.

It's beyond me why people are so worried that gay marriage will negatively affect the institution. It's the heterosexuals they should be worried about. You simply have to fear for the future of marriage given the current zeitgeist. It's as if the subtle cultural signals are that only the stupid dull people stay married. The really fun opinion leaders mix it up a bit with at least a couple of marriages and a number of affairs. Maybe we should just face facts and change the marriage vows themselves – or invent 'Marriage Lite' where, rather than promising to have and to hold forever for better or worse, we come up with a form of words that more accurately describes the situation. Something along the lines of: 'I promise to have a couple of kids and live with you for twenty years. At that stage I'll review the situation. If you've become a bit boring and flabby I reserve the right to nick off elsewhere.'

I can't help but think of how radically the times have changed. My mum tells a wonderful story about her mum, Granny Vi. Granny Vi was a gorgeous woman – born, lived and died in the same house. In all her years she never had central heating or a fridge. Hardworking and uncomplaining, Granny Vi was what we used to call the salt of the earth. I don't believe she ever said a bad word about anyone.

A few years ago Mum took over a video of *Pretty Woman* for them to watch. Mum had loved the film and thought Granny Vi would enjoy it too. And indeed, Granny Vi sat on the edge of her seat, not uttering a word, and peered intently at the screen for the whole two hours watching the romance blossom between Julia Roberts and Richard Gere. When the film was over Mum turned to her and asked what she thought.

Granny Vi looked at Mum and said, 'So he didn't go back to his wife then?'

Brilliant.

I had to go and re-rent the film as I didn't realise Richard Gere's character even *had* a wife. Sure enough, less than two minutes into the film Gere has a thirty-second telephone call during which he breaks up with 'Jessica'. We don't see her and it's not even established that they are married, but she is identified as his partner and to Granny Vi that was clearly synonymous with her being his wife. She had subsequently spent the whole film earnestly hoping for a reconciliation even though Jessica is never mentioned again. It shows a rather different view of commitment and the concept of lifelong partnership.

I'm not saying Granny Vi's view of the world is right, but thank the Lord she passed away before she got a chance to witness *Keeping Up With the Kardashians* or read the *Huffington Post*.

25

The Wild Rover

It would be fair to say I am a bizarre mix of extremely 'risk averse' when it comes to things like debt, and absurdly 'risk comfortable' when it comes to other areas of my life, such as career management. After all, taking a break in your career isn't so rare – but three times?

Looking back with the benefit of hindsight, it's difficult to explain how risky the first time was. As it turned out, I wrote a book that sold well and then got another good job. But at the time I didn't know that was going to happen. When I asked my brother what hope there was that I'd ever get a job again he replied, 'Two hopes – Bob Hope and No Hope.' It was hard to disagree. I was a fat, forty-year-old, alcoholic unemployed ad man without a publisher, agent or job offer in sight. It was an *incredibly* scary situation. But it turned out to be the best thing that ever happened to me.

This experience of the risk paying off (irrespective of whether it was because of pure luck or something else) has had a huge impact on me. Not just in my attitude towards taking risks in my career but in other areas as well, particularly with regard to creativity. I've been lucky to spend my entire career in a creative industry working alongside truly creative people. I love it, and I love them. But up until I lost my job, I had this deep unshakeable belief that I wasn't one of them. It just was an accepted part of my mental hardwiring that I didn't have the right to be creative. Or even the right to attempt to be.

At work this wasn't a problem. My role was always to be 'a suit'. It was the creative department's role to come up with the ideas and my job to sell them. I was fine with that. It was in my personal life that I came to realise that avoiding creativity was an issue that needed serious attention. For forty years I had just accepted that creative pursuits weren't for me. It wasn't my place to sing or draw or write. After all, I hadn't shown any particular aptitude for these activities and on the rare occasions when I attempted them my efforts were met with friendly derision. Standard behaviour, I'm sure, in many families and peer groups.

So, like thousands of others, the belief that I could indulge in creative pursuits was beaten out of me from an early age. I've since come to believe this is a tragedy, because being creative is an essential part of what it means to be fully human. It's bad for your soul to have no outlet for creative expression. I say this from personal experience: in recent years – emboldened by the success of taking risks in other areas of my life – I've thought, 'I'm going to take a risk and try these things anyway.' And the experience has been genuinely transformative, making me regret all those years where I'd ignored that part of myself.

I'm not talking here about pretending you're better than you really are at these pursuits; proper awareness of your limitations is vital. Nor am I suggesting you should expect other people to be interested in your efforts. I'm talking about *breaking the law that says you can only engage in creative pursuits if you're good at them.*

There are fantastic benefits to regularly expressing yourself creatively in the knowledge that you *aren't* particularly gifted. Sure it feels uncomfortable and a bit silly at first, but once you conquer your fear, ignore the outcome and disregard the need for any external affirmation of your efforts it feels natural. More than that, exploring my creative side has resulted in some of the most joyous moments of my life. I've often told my children, 'It doesn't matter how well you go as long as you have a go' when they've been nervous before a sporting match. The same rule applies when it comes to picking up that paintbrush or those drumsticks. The nineteenth-century essayist Sydney Smith put it slightly more articulately when he remarked, 'It is the greatest of all mistakes to do nothing because you can only do a little – do what you can.' Where the hell was he when I was at school?

When I started drawing the pleasure and satisfaction I got from even the lamest of pictures is hard to express. It made me feel like I was throwing off shackles that had been holding me down in all areas of my life. Just the simple act of daring to draw lifted my gaze above the humdrum to all the glorious possibilities in this world.

As one of my favourite writers, Michael McGirr, has said, 'The secret of being human is learning how to enjoy our limitations.' And that's the point. Awareness of your limitations shouldn't stop you trying. Nor should failure. In a way, it was what I was having to overcome when I learnt to cook. Even if I was crap at it I was determined to keep giving it a go.

It's so easy to fall into a life where you try nothing new and hide behind a computer screen. It's easy to read a cookbook instead of cooking or follow a talent show and never perform. But it's just so limiting and sad to be scared into never being able to try anything new or outside your comfort zone. I look back with shame on all those occasions when I have been part of the problem and humorously mocked others when they have dared to be creative.

Kate and I recently put two sculptures in our back garden. They are huge wooden pieces by a lovely and talented artist called Sasha Reid. Essentially, they are large trunks of wood mounted on steel legs with wide-open bright orange mouths cut into them. The works are entitled *Big Mouth* and the inspiration behind them came from Sasha repeatedly overhearing people walking past works of art and opining to their friends that 'I could have done that'. They serve as a wonderful reminder whenever I lose confidence in my right to write, draw, play music – or do anything creative – for fear of the criticism I will attract, to carry on regardless.

Some of my artwork

The world would be a far happier and more peaceful place if we were all a bit more generous with children and friends in these areas. Admittedly, though, you can go too far. My attitude in this area probably means my own kids will be put off it for life. I'm so keen that they don't have my early negative experience that I overcompensate and am always encouraging them to get involved in, or stick with, creative tasks. I can picture them in fifteen years' time sitting in their office saying to their co-workers, 'I was drawn to a career in accountancy after my father forced me to do five years of dance and saxophone lessons.'

But while it's important to avoid giving false praise, it's still possible to salute the effort. Next time someone tells you they have taken up a new pursuit, rather than taking the piss how about congratulating them instead?

This lesson was most powerfully brought home to me last year when Kate bought me a guitar for my birthday. I might not be able to tune the bloody thing or read music, but when I'm alone, bothering no one, I can strum away in a state of barely contained bliss. I have a couple of friends who *are* good at the guitar and just five minutes of messing around with them learning a few new songs can provide me with months of future enjoyment.

One of these friends, Andrew, asked me if I'd like to play in his band at a forthcoming gig. At first I was overwhelmed with all the old negative emotions – I'm crap at the guitar, I'll make a fool of myself, I'll fuck up his gig, people will laugh, etc., etc. But upon reflection I realised it would make a mockery of my creative philosophy if I fell at this hurdle. Besides, I was only going to be playing backing guitar on one three-chord song. So I said yes. Needless to say, the gig was fine, and for those four minutes of 'The Wild Rover' I was in heaven. I even *sang*. But the undisputed, never-to-be-beaten high spot of the night wasn't playing the guitar, or singing – or even on stage. No, it was at the beginning of the night as I was walking into the venue. The pub had put on bouncers for the night and when I arrived carrying my guitar one of them asked me, 'Mate, are you with the band?'

Rather than say, 'No, not really, the lead singer is a friend and he's let me play back-up guitar for one song,' I just said, 'Yes.'

And the wonderful thing is he didn't say, 'You? You've got to be kidding. You look like you should be sitting at a desk, not performing live music.' Instead he said, 'Okay, follow me. I'll show you to the stage.'

It took all my self-control to stop myself from giving him a hug.

My performance hardly qualifies me for an entry into the rock-and-roll hall of fame but I'm pretty certain that, however proficient I ever get on the guitar, it will be difficult to match the feeling I had on that first night.

26

North Head

While following a have-a-go philosophy with creative pursuits, in other areas I am far less casual. Never more so than with my running. If scales are essential for any weight-loss program, the best way to measure progress with running is to use a stopwatch. I, personally, love the honesty of the stopwatch. The time on your wrist at the end of a race is the time you ran. End of story.

In a quest to improve my running times after I left work, I wanted *proof* of improvement. Feeling great wasn't going to be enough. I wanted a running goal that was challenging but realistic, ongoing over the long term but not impossible to achieve.

After knocking things around in my mind for a few weeks I came upon what I believed was the perfect answer, resolving that in my fifties I would try to run a ten-kilometre road race every year *in a time that was under my age*. So, for example, in the year I turned fifty I wanted to do a ten-kilometre race in under fifty minutes; the year after, in less than fifty-one minutes and so on until I turned sixty. I would then devise a new set of targets for my sixties.

To a good runner my goal would sound almost laughably easy, but to me it was a considerable stretch because, as Kate sweetly maintains, I have deceptive pace – *I'm slower than I look*. The fastest time I have ever done ten kilometres in is 49:54. The problem is that I was twenty-seven years old at the time.

For the past few years every road race I've done has been with one or more of my kids so I've walked all or most of them. In the last ten-kilometre race I'd done by myself I'd clocked up the hilariously inept time of 81:32. That's the warp speed of a kilometre in eight minutes, or seven and a half kilometres per hour. Watch your back Usain Bolt, Nigel Marsh is in town. So it was fair to say I needed to deliver some serious improvement if I was to do ten consecutive kilometres at five minutes per kilometre by the time I turned fifty.

For me an essential step in any challenge is to make an accurate, honest assessment of the situation I'm in – as per my weight-loss attempts. I need to know precisely where I'm starting from to have any chance of getting anywhere meaningful.

In order to see where I was at with my running I decided to call the Sydney Striders, a running club that holds timed ten-kilometre races throughout the year. Participating in one of their runs would allow me to get an up-to-date benchmark from which to work. Then, after I got my base time, I'd use the remaining two years until my fiftieth birthday to make sure I was properly in shape to start my decade of sub-age races.

It turned out that the next race on the Sydney Striders' schedule was to take place at North Head, overlooking Sydney Harbour, early on a Saturday morning in September. It would be my first race since the beginning of my year off so would provide a good line in the sand regarding my new life.

I signed up online and decided that the moment I pressed the button to enter would mark the official confirmation of my latest goal. So, I had two weeks to get myself prepared. It wasn't long enough to do anything about my fitness, but at least I had enough time to prepare mentally, not to mention buy the right kit. Hence to the sports shop, where I bought some new runners and also took the plunge and bought a heart-rate monitor. Though I'm ashamed to admit it, until I bought my own heart monitor I thought anyone who wore one was a pretentious wanker. However, I wanted to do this right.

The helpful lady in the shop showed me how to use the monitor and, taking into account my weight, height and age, even set the all-important 'in zone' range measures for me so I would know if I was running too fast (fat chance) or too slow. My limit was one hundred and twenty-one heartbeats at the lower end and one hundred and fifty-two at the upper end.

That evening I went for a run to check out my new toy, staying out for twenty-five minutes and pushing myself slightly harder than usual. Afterwards, I was pleasantly surprised to learn that my average heart rate during the run was one hundred and thirty-one, while my maximum was one hundred and forty-six. Nothing to shout about, but within the target range.

The Sydney Striders have a rule that all entrants have to do a ten-kilometre race in under an hour and, due to my level of fitness at the time, I was concerned. I desperately didn't want to be disqualified in my very first training race, so I went for another couple of training runs before the race, each time managing to stay within my ideal heart-rate zone.

On the morning of the race I woke up nervous but excited and set off early. As I parked the car at North Head the sun was coming up over the horizon and I was stunned by the beautiful vista of the heads themselves, the gorgeous blue sky, the top of the Harbour Bridge and the Manly ferries crossing the sparkling water.

When the other runners started to arrive, they were all very friendly and welcoming, though it was clear they couldn't really be described as casual runners. They had the lean athletic bodies and skimpy kit that are hallmarks of the serious runner. I felt slightly embarrassed parading around in my old Bath rugby shirt and baggy shorts.

Looking at the course for the race I saw it was two five-kilometre loops. The lady who gave me my race number informed me that the front runners (or the 'greyhounds', as she called them) would do the race in thirty or so minutes. Fuck me, I thought, that was seriously fast and meant that if it took me over sixty minutes, not only would I be disqualified, I would risk being lapped as well.

A steely determination descended upon me. I might not be very fit or very fast, but I resolved to die from exhaustion rather than be lapped or disqualified. No longer having an office to go to or a business card to flash can do strange things to you . . .

The race started at 7 am and as we all gathered behind the start line I noticed one runner had a flag strapped to his back with '45' on it.

'Excuse me, mate, what's that thing?' I asked.

'I'm the forty-five-minute pace marker,' he replied.

'What does that mean?'

'Follow me and you'll do the race in forty-five minutes,' he said.

'How on earth do you know you're going at that pace?' I asked.

'Mate, it's what I do.' He looked at me quizzically.

'Oh, of course,' I said. 'Is there a sixty-minute flag bloke?'

This time the guy's look was more pitying than quizzical. 'No, mate. But there's a fifty-five-minute marker. There, near the back.' He pointed.

'Thanks,' I replied and moved off to stand behind the fifty-five-minute marker.

As the minutes ticked down before the start, I decided to ignore my previously decided-upon race plan of 'Slow, Steady, Strong, Sprint'. Instead I would focus on doing everything in my power to keep the fifty-five-minute flag in my sights to ensure I reached the finish line well within the hour.

The gun went and everyone raced off a little too fast for my liking. However, I gritted my teeth, picked up my pace and settled in on the fifty-five-minute bloke's shoulder. I had set my stopwatch on the gun and checked it to see if it was working – all good. I'd been told there were signs at every kilometre so not only were there flag blokes to help, you could also track your time using the signs. I just wanted to get to the first kilometre marker in under six minutes so I'd know I was within the bare minimum necessary pace to avoid disqualification – and being lapped.

I hadn't warmed up before the race and was finding the going a bit hard, so I focused on my shoes and concentrated on my breathing. After four minutes I started to keep an eye out for the upcoming marker. I was still finding it hard going but felt confident I had it under control. At five minutes I sped up slightly in anticipation of the marker. To no effect. Six minutes came and went and I still hadn't seen the one-kilometre marker. I sped up again but a couple of minutes later it dawned on me that maybe there *wasn't* a one-kilometre marker. My pace and breathing were now all over the place from my early exertion.

Relax, Nigel, you're doing fine. Now where's that fifty-five minute flag?

I looked ahead and couldn't see it. I weaved to the left and right, scanning all the bobbing heads and shoulders, but no flag.

A wave of self-doubt hit me.

You may think you're doing fine, Nigel, but you're so out of shape you've not even done two kilometres and the fifty-five-minute marker is already out of sight. You're clearly not going as fast as you think you are.

I glanced to my right and was shocked to see an elderly gentleman running along beside me. He was slightly hunched over, and while his head was entirely bald, he had an enormous amount of grey hair sprouting out from the chest and shoulders of his skimpy running singlet. He couldn't have been a day under seventy.

Fuck me ragged. Have some self-respect, Nige. You're being overtaken by an octogenarian.

Feeling slightly panicked, I lengthened my stride to try to stop him pulling ahead.

Right, you tub of lard, get a grip. You've probably ballsed up this race already but there is no way you're going to let this bloke beat you. He's clearly thirty years older than you and he's not complaining. Your first race was always going to be a bit of a discovery process. You're obviously not as fit or as fast as you should be but that's fine. This is a long-term goal. You've got a couple of years to prepare. Forget sixty minutes. Forget being lapped. Ignore everything else – just stick with the old bloke.

Having set my new target I started to feel calmer. *Just stick with the old bloke. Just stick with the old bloke.* I repeated this to myself like a mantra with every step.

Damn me, though, if he wasn't a tough one, despite his slightly frail appearance. He simply didn't slow down – ever. In fact, I swear he sped up on the inclines. No matter; I grimly stuck with him regardless.

By the finish of the first five-kilometre lap I was in serious trouble. Not only was my breathing all over the place, but I felt light-headed and not a little like I was going to be sick. But at least I was still on the old bloke's shoulder.

Come on, you pussy, you're halfway there. Nothing is so bad that you can't stand it for thirty minutes. Man up. Just stick with the old bloke.

I glanced across at him in the hope he was tiring, but he looked the same. Plod, plod, plod, at exactly the same pace.

My shirt wet with sweat and my left foot and knee hurting dreadfully, I stuck with him for the next few minutes, pounding down the road by his side for what seemed an eternity. We seemed to being going much faster than my normal pace but we still hadn't caught the fifty-five-minute marker, which I'd been keeping a constant eye out for. And then I saw a bollard with nine kilometres written on it.

Nine kilometres! I was almost there. My spirits lifted. I felt a little euphoric. As if the old bloke could sense my renewed energy, he picked up his pace.

No worries, mate, I'm with you for the duration. You ain't got nothing. Bring it on.

Brilliant. I was mentally trash-talking a seventy-year-old.

It felt like I was sprinting. Hold on, I *was* sprinting.

Pick on someone your own age, Nige. No, fuck that – he's going down.

I ran as fast as I could and pulled away from him.

I'm leading the old bloke! I'm leading the old bloke!

My breath rasping loudly, my left knee in agony, sweat running into my eyes, I gave the last k everything I had and crossed the finish line a good ten metres ahead of the old guy, then immediately knelt in the bushes at the side of the road and retched painfully.

A few moments later I felt a hand on my shoulder and looked up to see the old bloke.

'Good race, mate,' he said with a friendly smile.

Why wasn't *he* retching?

'Thanks,' I said when I could catch my breath. 'You look like you've done this before.'

'Yep, haven't missed a race for years.'

'Really? What time do you usually do?'

'Mostly between forty-eight and fifty-two minutes. I was a bit slower today.'

What?! That's absurd. Did he just say between forty-eight and fifty-two? Talk about bad luck; I'd clearly picked the world's fastest old bloke to follow. That'd teach me to judge a book by its cover. But what about the fifty-five-minute flag? I wondered. What had happened to him? Then, looking back, I saw the fifty-five minute bloke crossing the finish line and suddenly it hit me. I hadn't been able to see fifty-five-minute man during the race *because I was ahead of him*. I'd just assumed he was so far in front I couldn't see him – it hadn't occurred to me he might be behind me. So what time had I done? I hadn't looked at my watch since I'd decided on the 'stick with the old bloke' strategy. Nor had I pressed the button at the finish line.

'Mate, what time did you do?' I asked.

'Fifty-three twenty.'

Fifty-three twenty? I'd only wanted to break sixty!

I glanced down and saw my stopwatch was still running. Taking out the time I'd spent being sick and talking, I must have come in at around fifty-three minutes!

I suddenly remembered the heart-rate monitor and pressed the button. It showed my average heart rate had been one hundred and sixty-three, my maximum one hundred and eighty-nine.

One hundred and eighty-nine! It didn't seem possible, or indeed sensible. But leaving aside the sprint at the end the simple fact of the matter was that I had unwittingly run for almost an hour at a consistent average pace of one hundred and sixty-three when my previous *maximum* rate was one hundred and fifty-two.

I don't know what that meant for my heart, but no wonder my left knee hurt.

Apart from not judging a book by its cover, I took another key lesson away from this, my benchmark race: it's amazing what you can achieve if you get your mental belief right. If someone had said to me that they wanted me to run at fifty-three-minute pace before the North Head ten-kilometre run I wouldn't have believed I could do it and would have slowed down when I'd started really hurting during the race. However, because I *thought* I was running at close to sixty-minute pace, when it really started to hurt I couldn't justify slowing down and just kept going instead. Same bloke, same level of fitness – just different mental backdrop.

It reminds me of the wonderful story about Roger Bannister breaking the four-minute-mile barrier. For decades people had been trying and failing to do this until finally Bannister made history with his now-famous Oxford run. Yet in the year after he broke the barrier close to two hundred people also went on to break it – *because they now believed it was possible.* I'm not equating my pathetic fifty-three-minute ten kilometres with Bannister's four-minute mile, but too often in life we limit what we think we can achieve. Then we live up (or down) to those beliefs. However, if you get your head right, raise your standards and change your limiting beliefs, it's truly remarkable what you can achieve in lots of areas of your life. Who knew, just maybe, with the right attitude, I might make a success of my third break from the office after all.

27

it's All About Me

Since I'd been working from home and Kate was the one going to the office we'd fallen into a routine of me driving her to the office every morning. It was one of the favourite parts of my day because it gave us a chance to spend some time alone and have a good conversation. Or so I thought.

One morning three months into this routine I noticed Kate seemed a bit quiet.

'Sweetheart, you haven't said a word,' I noted when she was silent after I'd finished what I thought was a particularly good story. 'Are you alright?'

'I'm fine,' she replied.

'No you're not, I can tell. What's wrong?'

'Nothing's wrong . . . Well, alright, actually there *is* something I've been meaning to discuss with you.'

'Thought so. Tell me.'

187

'The thing is, while I appreciate you driving me to work you know I also like to be quiet in the mornings, right?'

'What are you saying?'

'Well I don't mind you wittering on at me in car in the mornings – I quite like it as a sort of background noise – but I'd prefer it if I didn't have to respond or give any reaction. I'm not really listening, to be honest.'

Marvellous. But then again I suppose I could now view these car trips as useful practice for my one-way telephone conversations with my dad.

It's not the first time Kate has rumbled me. Only the week before we'd had an argument after I had rather pathetically whined about my lack of 'me-time'.

'It's *all* me-time with you, Nigel,' she scoffed.

'Not true,' I protested.

'Rubbish – you're always thinking about what you want to do.'

'You're making this up.'

'Really? When you go into a café with the kids, what's your first thought?'

'What do you mean?'

'Well my first thought is: "I wonder what they've got that's suitable for the kids." What's yours? Truthfully.'

I thought about it. And it hit me. *She's right*. When I reflected honestly on her question the awful truth was in that situation my first thought is usually 'I wonder what *I'm* going to have.'

Busted. I like to think my very next thought is what the kids might like, but all the same . . .

I might be able to fool some of the people some of the time, but I've never been able to fool my wife. In fact, I've lost count of the times Kate has said, 'You know, Nigel, it's not all about you.'

Which made it all the more satisfying on one particular occasion to be able to turn to her and say, 'Sweetheart, in this particular instance it truly *is* all about me.'

The occasion in question occurred in the wake of an email telling me that a well-known actor was keen to produce *Fat, Forty and Fired* as a play. And not only was he going to produce the play he was also going to direct and star in it. *No other character was going to be in it.* Just one man acting me on stage. Alone. For two hours.

I couldn't help but find the idea of the play rather thrilling. What's more, the theatre company was going to fly Kate and me first class across the country to sit in front-row seats on the opening night. Though I tried to be nonchalant about it all, I was totally excited about it and could hardly wait for my 'all about me' night to arrive. It wasn't just vanity fuelling my eagerness, but the possibility I might make a small amount of money from the production if it had a successful launch and then went on to tour other Australian capital cities. And the timing was perfect, with the opening night scheduled for four months after my last day in the office – about the time that I knew the reality of not having an office to go to or a salary to rely on would well and truly have begun to bite.

So it was with much excitement that I saw an email from the theatre company arrive in my inbox asking me to call them. Perhaps they wanted to upgrade our hotel? Or maybe they wanted me to make a speech before the opening performance? My head was fairly buzzing with all the delicious possibilities when I sat down with my morning coffee and made the call.

'Hi, Nigel here. You asked me to ring.'

'Yes. It's bad news I'm afraid.'

'Oh, I'm sorry. Rehearsals not going well?'

'No, they've been going extremely well, actually. It's not that. It's . . . it's . . . There's no easy way to say this: Dermot passed away last night.'

'He did what?'

'He passed away. He died. Dermot's dead.'

'Are you sure?' I asked.

'Yes, sadly. I spent the night with his grieving family.'

I resisted the temptation to ask them to double check the corpse.

'Oh, that's awful,' I said when I'd regained my composure. 'I'm really sorry. Please pass on my sincerest condolences to everyone.'

We spoke for a few more minutes before agreeing we'd talk at a more appropriate time about the practical ramifications of this terrible personal tragedy.

The follow-up call merely served to confirm what I'd suspected would come to pass. There would be no play. No national tour. No money. And, of course, no it's-all-about-me opening night either.

This episode made me think that we spend far too much time these days moaning about the challenges of getting old. It's as if a switch is flicked when we turn fifty that makes us complain about everything. *Grumpy Old Men* and *Grumpy Old Women* videos sell in their thousands. And I get that it's fun to watch and identify with the grumpy old people as they rant humorously about the downsides of old age. But Dermot's death at the age of sixty had me thinking we should actually feel enormous gratitude for the privilege of *having* an old age. Needing to wear glasses, finding it difficult to hear properly when there's any background noise or any of the other old-age irritations are a mere bagatelle when you consider the alternative: Dermot's alternative.

With the proper planning and perspective old age can be the happiest time of your life.

Dermot's untimely demise also reminded me that my darling Granny Vi was right about not counting chickens before they've hatched. As well as the hope that the play might provide some income, one of my secret plans was to financially provide for my family during my year off with proceeds from the film production of *Fat, Forty and Fired*. I'd sold the rights to a well-respected film producer a couple of years earlier and I'd had sporadic fantasies about huge royalty cheques ever since.

I've since learnt that glaciers move faster than most films take to produce. So, despite all the talk of potentially being played by actors such as Steve Carrell or Robert Downey Jr, I've begun to realise that if a film ever eventuates at all I'm likely to have long since seen off my fifties before I see any cheque.

Relying on a film or play to fund my latest hiatus was little better than playing the lottery. And as I used to regularly say in the office, Hope Isn't a Plan. It might fuel a few enjoyably self-indulgent daydreams, but it was unlikely to cover my year away from the office.

28

Speed Limits

Having put the Hope Strategy behind me, my thoughts returned to exactly how Kate and I were going to be able to keep paying the monthly bills. A couple of years ago I was asked by an interviewer what my ultimate career ambition was. I surprised myself when, without any pause for thought, I replied, 'To be paid a fortune to go to work three days a week and be myself.' Rereading it later I remember thinking it wasn't actually such a bad answer.

It's never been my burning ambition to be the global CEO of Mega Corp Inc. Nor would I want to sit around and do nothing. I'd much rather contribute to the world by using whatever talents I may have, while at the same time living a balanced life with my family. By this definition, if you leave the 'be paid a fortune' bit aside, public speaking is pretty close to being one of my ultimate jobs. Which is great, because it turned out that speaking became my main source of income during this time-out period in my life.

I love making a meaningful connection with people when I'm speaking at an event or conference. My personal mantra is to Entertain, Elevate, Educate. As an objective I find it much more motivating than double-digit growth or whatever other arid tosh we're told to chase in the corporate world.

I have a rule never to give a speech on something I don't care about. So while I might be capable of giving a speech on, say, trends in luxury tourism, it would be better to book someone else because my heart simply wouldn't be in it. My rule about having to care about the subject I talk about ensures I never give less than a hundred per cent when I do a gig. It doesn't mean I'm always right, however. Indeed part of my love for speaking work is the learning process. If someone can change my mind on any issue I talk about – that's fine. I've no problems with amending my position in the face of compelling argument or evidence.

Over the years I have gone out of my way to challenge people to correct me on one particular thing above all others – my 'rules' to guaranteed business success. I started compiling this list of rules for business success a few years ago out of sheer frustration at all the management fads that companies fall for. It's as if company executives, and the business media, have no corporate memory. They are forever falling for the latest miracle answer or author who claims to have the secret answer to commercial success. Before I put forward my list in any speech I do, I usually rant about how rubbish I find most business books (as I've already done a few chapters ago). I then say that the answers to business success are simple, have always been the same and will never change.

Much as it might upset the HR experts, I cite the example of those employee manuals we've all seen. Huge thick documents endlessly discussing people's needs when in reality people only have three needs in a work-organisation context. They want to know who they report to and what's expected of them, and they want regular feedback. Be honest. That's what you want, isn't it? But that appears too simple – and would result in too thin a manual – so we get the huge tomes instead.

Finally, before revealing my list, I challenge everyone in the audience to write to me afterwards if they feel there is an omission or indeed any items on the list that should be left off.

There are six rules on the list:

1. Satisfy your customers.
2. Motivate your employees and colleagues.
3. Work hard.
4. Behave consistently.
5. Prepare for the future.
6. Control costs.

I'd be genuinely fascinated to meet the business leader who claims to be following all six rules whose business is still failing.

For two years no one suggested an amendment to the list. Not one. It wasn't that people didn't write to me. They did. In their hundreds. But all I got was vigorous agreement. People wrote asking for the list again or to tell me how ardently they agreed. Others wrote to tell me how much they hated the fact that they had to pretend to be excited when their company was gripped by the latest business fad. And how they wished they could just be left alone to concentrate on the stuff that they knew really worked. The stuff on the list.

Then one day in 2009 I received an email from a senior female executive who'd attended one of my speeches. She wrote: 'Nigel, I've been thinking about your list ever since the conference and I hope you don't mind, but I do have an inclusion: "Maintain your integrity."'

Well, it may have taken a while for someone to put forward a suggestion, but it was worth the wait.

Maintain your integrity.

Brilliant. She's right. I like to think it's covered by my fourth rule, but maybe it does deserve a rule of its own.

Trouble is, 'maintain your integrity' is wonderful advice in theory, but in the real world of corporate shenanigans it can be hard to do. However good your intentions, it can sometimes be so damn difficult to know *what* the right thing to do is.

I have found it a constant challenge throughout my career to know with absolute certainty what the right course of action is in a given situation. Still do. It's incredibly important to me to maintain my own sense of personal integrity within the business environment, but the more senior you get the more challenging this becomes because you're faced with more and more complex issues. Everything is interrelated, nothing is simple and every decision seems to have an unforeseen consequence. This is the reason many leaders look to the laws of the land or industry codes of practice to guide them. Yet to my mind codes and laws are part of the ethical problem, not the solution.

My thinking on this matter was crystallised by the situation I found myself in when I arrived in Australia to take up my first CEO role. I discovered soon after I started that the firm I'd been asked to run was in truly awful shape. Indeed, it quickly became apparent that the only reason I'd got the job was that they hadn't been able to find anyone in Australia stupid enough to take it. The situation was so bad that people were being 'let go' every week. It was clear that the only way to get the firm out of the mess it was in was to win some new clients. Fast.

Now the way you get new clients in the advertising industry is to 'pitch' for them. This is an extremely competitive form of beauty parade where ten or so companies are asked to sell themselves and their ideas to the prospective client. After these presentations the list is whittled down to four companies and *then you do it all over again.* Often yet another hurdle is added in which the final two agencies battle it out over a further stage before the contract is finally awarded. It is an expensive and draining process in which the chances of winning are by definition one in ten or one in four. Those are not good odds given the upfront non-refundable investment of time, energy and money.

Prior to coming to Australia I'd done literally hundreds of pitches, so I was well aware of the hard work necessary to successfully turn the firm's fortunes around. That is, until I got a phone call during my third week in the role.

'I'd like to speak to Nigel Marsh,' a male voice said.

'Speaking,' I replied.

'Ah, excellent – I've heard about you, Nigel. I think we'd work well together. I'd like to give you our advertising account.'

'Er . . . really? That's wonderful,' I said uncertainly, thinking it sounded suspiciously like a wind-up from one of my mates. 'What do you do?' I asked.

'Run a bordello,' he replied.

Now until that day I'd thought Bordello was a red wine. As the conversation continued, however, it became clear this chap wasn't talking about red wine. Far from being a wind-up, this prospective client seriously wanted our firm to help promote the new state-of-the-art brothel he was building in the centre of the city. As far as I could make out from his breathless description, 'state of the art' meant 'themed rooms' but, whatever, it *was* a huge new establishment.

The fees for our involvement if we took on the brief would be substantial and, more importantly, would mean I could forgo the next couple of redundancies we had planned. The effect on agency morale of an immediate new win would be great. And all without a sodding pitch.

After concluding the conversation I went to chat to my management team. I like to work collaboratively and clearly this bizarre situation warranted proper discussion before we committed to anything. When I explained the matter to my colleagues the response was split. My creative partners were excited about the potential to do some edgy, eye-catching work (I also think I heard one of them whisper something enthusiastically about 'store visits'). Others were horrified I'd even raised it with them as a possibility because to them it was unthinkable we'd touch such a contract. Personally, I was yet to make up my mind. On the one hand it wasn't really the type of business I joined the industry to promote, but on the other hand I couldn't help but be preoccupied with the next round of redundancies.

After fielding opinions I decided we should get the prospective client in to the agency to explain the brief before making up our minds. I suggested we put in place a 'UN veto' – basically agreeing that if, after hearing what he had to say, *anyone* on the management team didn't want us to do it then the agency would decline to be involved.

I called the man back and fixed a date for him and a colleague to meet with us. On the day itself I was a little nervous. At the risk of coming across like a choirboy, I've never actually been to a brothel before – let alone met the owner of one – so I had no idea what to expect.

Any prejudices I might have had were immediately challenged when the bordello owner and his colleague turned up in our reception. Both were well presented, polite and professional. This wasn't a joke to them – it was their livelihood. They took it every bit as seriously as our other more mainstream clients took their businesses.

I showed them to our boardroom and introduced them to my partners. After some small talk they set about explaining the brief.

The first part of the brief was, in summary: 'If you are a fat and lonely businessman who can't get laid, come on down to Shagtastic' – not the real name, I hasten to add – 'and it's a sure thing.'

The second part of the brief *was* a surprise because it was about recruiting staff. Our client wanted us to advertise in poor rural areas to try to attract young women in dead-end jobs. Essentially the message would be: 'Bored stacking shelves at the local supermarket? Fed up with only earning $x an hour? Well, come on down to the big city and work at Shagtastic. Not only will you earn $XXX an hour, but you'll see the bright lights and meet some fascinating men.'

After the meeting ended and the clients had left the building the management team had a rather emotional discussion. Ultimately, having taken everyone's opinions into consideration, I had to make the final call. How could I possibly be involved in such a thing? I asked myself. If I wouldn't be happy for my own daughters to be influenced by the sort of ad campaign we'd need to conceive, how on earth could I justify trying to influence someone else's child? Did the fact I was never going to meet the people it affected make it somehow alright? I didn't think so. Who the hell did I think I was even to call the meeting in the first place? To cut a long story short we declined the account, another agency took the contract and we went ahead with the next round of redundancies.

The point of this story is that in this instance, laws and codes were *utterly useless* in helping us make a decision because the brothel was entirely legal. Advertising it was entirely legitimate according to the stringent advertising industry codes. It was factually correct that a number of accommodating women would act pleased to see you if you visited Shagtastic.

My conclusion is that laws and codes are like speed limits. They may contribute to your decision-making on an issue, but only by establishing where the floor is, not the ceiling. By analogy, if you see a road sign indicating a speed limit of fifty kilometres per hour, you are being told you can go fifty kilometres per hour without breaking any rules. Imagine seeing the same road sign at a time when it's getting dark, the road is icy, a school bus loaded with excited six-year-olds has pulled up on one side of the road and an ice-cream van has started to play its music on the opposite side. In these circumstances you are *still* allowed to go fifty kilometres per hour – but only a moron would suggest it's a good idea to do so. Any right-thinking person would slow down to below the speed limit. Rather than following the letter of the law in this instance, you should obviously exercise your own judgement.

So it is with laws and codes in business, which encourage people to look elsewhere for moral guidance when in reality it is their own moral compass they should refer to. Used in the wrong way, laws and codes encourage people to forget they even *have* a moral compass – they enable them to make decisions about difficult issues purely on the basis of what is 'allowed'. My contention is that business leaders should be *personally* mindful about the ethics of their company.

After the brothel incident I developed a simple system to judge the acceptability of my future business actions. Whenever

I had to judge whether my firm should or shouldn't do something I didn't ask, 'Is it allowed?' but 'Would I be happy if what we are about to do were to affect the people I most love in the world?' It's important to project onto people or things we love to avoid the inbuilt mechanism many of us have that enables us to fool ourselves that we are too clever to be duped by marketers.

Imagine if a few years back any of those bankers had asked themselves, 'Would I be happy selling this toxic subprime mortgage stock to my mother?' instead of 'Am I *allowed* to sell it?' If they had, we might have avoided the worst of the GFC.

So my recommendation is, rather than the speed-limits view of morality, we would do well to adapt the age-old 'do unto others' rule. Whether you use this particular method or not, you can't be a good leader if you haven't got *some* method of tapping into your own moral compass – as opposed to relying on the ones society has instituted in its laws and codes.

One of the undoubted advantages of having left the office environment again was the welcome break from dealing with such thorny ethical dilemmas. That's not to say, however, I didn't have challenges of a different sort . . .

29

Washing-Up Liquid and Firm Tofu

As the months passed by after I left work the family settled into a new routine. From my perspective it was heaven. I viewed every day I didn't have to go into the office in the city as both a gift and a victory.

In some ways it was like one of those role-swap TV shows. For the past ten years I'd been the one who went to work to earn a wage and Kate had been on her own treadmill of looking after four young children with all the cooking, cleaning, loving encouragement and other things that involved. Now our roles were reversed, with Kate putting on her business suit and venturing into the corporate world.

Initially Kate found it a bit of a shock. The first day she forgot her purse, the second day her computer password, day three her knickers, and on day four she actually parked outside the school and was gaily walking to the canteen before she realised something was amiss. However, she soon adjusted and got back into the swing of it and now I was the one standing at the door in my dressing gown waving goodbye to a besuited partner.

One morning, six months into my new life, I was checking my daily to-do list as I always did before sitting down to write. A year before, this list would have been a multi-paged epic made up of important-sounding things like 'Call New York about acquisition' and 'Finalise budget presentation with CFO'. On this particular morning the largely blank piece of paper had the following two items:

1. Washing-up liquid
2. Firm tofu

That's it. There was no number three. Role swap indeed.

One of the adjustments I'd had to make during this particular hiatus was that grocery shopping could no longer be left solely to Kate. I didn't mind this, even though I don't particularly enjoy shopping. The reason I didn't mind was because the way Kate shops drives me up the wall. And the *results* of her shopping can make me want to lie down in a quiet darkened room. The latest drive-me-up-the-wall incident had occurred when Kate had headed to the shops to buy a rice cooker. Our old one had died a few months before but, being careful with our dollars and cents, we'd decided to wait until the sales to replace it.

The department store Kate intended to buy our new rice cooker from is barely two kilometres from where we live and has underground parking, so I expected her to be home in under an hour.

'Hi, sweetheart – what took you so long?' I asked when Kate finally appeared, looking slightly flustered, three hours later.

'Nothing – I was just deciding that's all,' she replied, a tad defensively.

'No worries. Let's get the thing out of its box and christen it. I've got a vegetable curry all ready to go.'

'Er . . . I didn't get a rice cooker,' Kate said.

'What's in that box then?' I asked.

'A summer dress,' she replied sheepishly.

'A summer dress *in a box*?' I queried.

'And a bedside lamp,' she said.

'But you went to get a rice cooker,' I pointed out.

'Yes, but these were on sale. And they're both gorgeous. Wait there a second and I'll show you.'

'But, darling, it's winter – and we already have a perfectly good bedside lamp. Two, in fact . . .' But I knew further debate was futile. Though she had planned to get a rice cooker she'd come back with a summer dress and a lamp. That's the way it rolls when Kate goes shopping.

My approach to shopping is at the opposite end of the spectrum. I don't view it as a recreational activity to be enjoyed. To my mind it's a functional exercise that has to be hurried through in the minimum time humanly possible. Nothing is ever bought that's not on the list. Nothing is even *looked at* that's not on the list.

I'm secretly trying to indoctrinate the kids into my way of shopping instead of Kate's. For a start it will save them thousands of dollars, and hours, in later life, but quite apart from that it makes them excellent helpers. My learn-to-cook project had been progressing fabulously. Not all the results I put on the table were fabulous, but the project as a whole was proving wonderfully rewarding in a myriad ways. And, increasingly, I'd started to rope the kids in to both help me cook and shop for the ingredients. In some ways it provided an even better one-on-one experience than the Dad's Trips. I'd pick one of them to go to the shops with me on a Sunday morning in preparation for 'Dad's dinner' that night and we'd march into the shop each with our own separate list and see who could get to the checkout with the required items in their basket first. On one occasion Grace and I went through both our lists *within 10 minutes.* Admittedly neither of us got a nice dress, or a lamp, but we sure as hell got home in under an hour.

30

Twenty-eight Red Roses

It hasn't happened for a while but last week, following an after-dinner speech, I got a Dead Fish. It never ceases to amaze me. You're introduced to someone then put out your hand in greeting but, rather than shaking it, they merely *place* their hand in yours. Lifelessly. As if it were a dead fish. It's all very awkward. And slightly rude.

I find the Dead Fish even more offputting than Space Invaders, namely those people who insist on standing too close to you when you're having a conversation. However, I do prefer the Dead Fish to those idiots who crush your hand rather than shake it. We've all met them. In some misguided attempt to establish authority or compensate for something they squeeze your hand with all their strength. I can almost understand this occurring in an alpha-male competitive situation, like politicians squaring off during an election or boxers meeting at a pre-fight press conference. However, in normal life it completely perplexes me. I've seen grown men do it to my *thirteen-year-old son*. And to my fifty-year-old aunt. What the hell are they trying to prove? I've started to confront it rather than suffer in silence.

'Oww – you really hurt my hand then,' I'll say.

'Pardon?' they say.

'Just then I found it unpleasantly painful when you shook my hand. You squeezed it so hard my knuckles hurt.'

'Oh, sorry, mate,' they always reply.

'That's alright – just thought I'd mention it as I'm sure you wouldn't want to go around hurting people.'

The giver of the Dead Fish at the dinner was actually a rather well-known personality whose public image is in stark contrast to a Dead-Fish merchant. He's actually a bit of an action hero. Strange. But then again I'm told that people who have to shake a lot of hands in their line of work are disproportionately prone to giving the Dead Fish. A properly given handshake – along with a bit of eye contact – establishes a spark of authentic human connection, and if you're in the fame game that can come to be the last thing you want.

For the first forty years of my life I rarely met anyone genuinely famous. I did bump into a few notable actors and directors because of my chosen career, but these meetings were usually fleeting and never regular. Since *Fat, Forty and Fired* was published and I started getting regular public-speaking gigs,

I've crossed paths with prime ministers, rock stars, Hollywood actors, adventurers, writers, sporting legends, business icons, self-help gurus, comedians, TV personalities – even astronauts. And, truth be told, with rare exception they have all been somehow unsatisfactory occasions.

Don't get me wrong. Invariably the well-known people I have met have been polite and nice and all their achievements remain extremely impressive. Still, meeting them was inevitably a letdown, bringing to mind the old English saying 'No man is a hero to his valet'. I've discovered it's better to admire famous people from afar.

The thing is, you already know why these people are famous. If you think about it, when you see them outside their natural fame habitat (of, say, being on stage or in a sporting stadium) it's hardly surprising you're not going to be wildly impressed. They aren't famous for making small talk; they're famous for swimming fast or performing great songs or whatever. You're peeking behind the façade and that is rarely a rewarding activity. Like peeking behind the set of a Wild West town in a cowboy film – you're only ever going to see the scaffolding that holds the wooden walls up.

I'll never forget the response of one young female journalist after interviewing Martin Luther King. 'I didn't know he smoked,' were the first words she blurted out to her startled editor. You learn new things and those things are by definition unlikely to surprise you in a good way. I mean, if you were lucky enough to meet Madonna how could it be anything but a letdown? You already know all her best songs, body and videos from her heyday. If you were with her in person tomorrow I guarantee you'd come away thinking, 'Gosh, her hands are very wrinkly' or 'She was a bit aloof.' Not that this makes her any less remarkable a person or artist. Nor do I think famous people are to blame or have in any way misled us here. It's our fault for projecting unrealistic hopes and desires onto them. Nevertheless, it remains a fact that famous people are likely to be disappointing up close.

I have come to the opposite conclusion about 'normal' people who aren't in the public eye and don't do anything that society deems as remarkable. One of the central beliefs of the Quakers is that there is a little bit of God in everyone, which is a beautiful notion. Sometimes this little bit can be hard to find, but you can usually uncover it with the appropriate effort. I've found that if you ask the right questions everyone has a fascinating story. These people aren't famous, so by definition anything new you find about them isn't likely to disappoint – it's likely to be interesting. Or impress. Or be moving. Or help you grow. It's the direct opposite of the famous syndrome.

During my time in advertising I always tried to get to know my colleagues as people rather than executives. And time and time again I was stunned and enriched by the stories this process revealed. That quiet person sitting in the IT department whom you might have unfairly written off as a techy dweeb has often got the most astonishing life story if you could only be bothered to listen.

In my last role I had a colleague whose job was to do the firm's public relations work. Pressures of work being what they were I didn't get around to taking her to lunch for over a year. When I finally did I wanted to be true to my philosophy of 'person not executive' so I asked questions about her life away from the office.

'So how are those two kids?' I asked.

'Actually, I've got three kids, Nigel,' she replied.

I was embarrassed. 'Oh God, Lynda, I'm sorry. How crass of me. I could have sworn you said you had two.'

'No need to apologise,' she said. 'I told you I had two.'

'Why did you do that?' I asked.

'It's a long story.'

'Good. I like long stories.'

'Really?'

'Try me.'

'Oh, alright. I can't believe I'm telling you this. It's not that interesting. Okay, do you know how old I am?'

'Nope. And you needn't tell me.'

'Well a while ago, a long while ago, when I was at college, I fell pregnant. My family was mortified. It was another time. Things were viewed differently then. I was sent away from home for my pregnancy. And when I had the baby it was immediately taken away from me.'

'Blimey, Lynda, that's awful,' I said.

'Yeah, not great,' she agreed.

'What happened then?' I asked.

'Life continued. I grieved, but you had no choice back then but to just get on with things.'

'And you never met your child? I'm sorry, do you mind me asking – was it a boy or a girl?'

'Boy.'

'And you never met him?'

'No. Not for twenty-eight years. After twenty-seven years I got an email from someone saying he was my son.'

'Must have got your attention.'

'I'll say. It was done through the proper channels. We swapped a few emails. It was all rather shattering and emotional. I couldn't trust myself to talk to him on the phone. We eventually agreed to meet.'

'Amazing. Where?'

'At Melbourne Airport. I was terrified. Standing there blubbing like a baby in the arrivals hall. There were so many deep emotions. It was complex. And raw. It had been such a long time and I wondered what on earth he'd think of me. I had no idea how he'd feel and act when he met me in person. I had no idea how I'd hold up.'

'And how was it?'

'He turned up carrying twenty-eight red roses. He kissed me on the cheek and said, "These are for all the Mother's Days I've missed."'

Jeez. If that's a story she calls 'not that interesting', I'd love to hear one she thinks is gripping. Lynda and her son have gone on to develop a loving and strong relationship and remain close to this day.

Funny old game, normal life. It's not just that the people in it are always more fascinating than high-profile celebs – it's that there's invariably more to learn from them. As well as being incredibly moved while I listened to Lynda's tale I realised it was the perfect story to prove that it's *never* too late to connect with your kids. Even if you think you're the worst example of a neglectful corporate father and have blown your chance of ever building a meaningful relationship with them, I believe you *can* change and you *can* make a difference. I'm not saying you have to take a year off like I have, but even the smallest change in attitude and approach can have the most amazing effects. I've seen men transform their lives and relationships almost overnight with little more than the sincere determination to be more mindful and considerate of their loved ones. You might not get twenty-eight roses in return, but I promise you the effort will be well worth it all the same.

31

Running to Fat

Six weeks into the 10.11 by 10.11 Wedding Cake Island weight-loss challenge it was time to check on our progress.

Put it this way: it had been a slow start. All four of us were behind schedule. Louise was even half a pound heavier than when she had first started. Not good.

The rest of us were lighter but still failing to lose a pound a week. I had lost five pounds, but was furious with myself for not having stayed on track. Call it delusion or determination, but I still had absolutely no doubt I was going to meet the target. I just didn't want to get there in a diet cliché of starving myself in the last two weeks.

Two lessons were coming through loud and clear six weeks in. The first was that in my case the correlation between my actions and my weight was pure. I *never* failed to lose weight when I stayed on track. I *never* failed to put it on when I lapsed. There were never any surprise results when I weighed myself and found I was five pounds heavier or five pounds lighter than I thought I was going to be. If I was honest with myself, I always knew when I stood on the scales which way it was going to go.

I did, however, make a new and enormously useful discovery from those first six weeks: like thousands of others before me, I had fallen into the trap of placing too much importance on the exercise side of the weight-loss equation.

True, there are two aspects that are essential to weight loss – energy in versus energy out. Energy in is food and drink, energy out is exercise. A lot of people in developed societies focus on exercise rather than reducing food intake as a means to weight loss. I know I do.

It was a painful lesson, but I'd come to realise it is fundamentally flawed thinking. Even though I see exercise as an essential part of a balanced, happy, healthy life and intend to keep doing regular exercise for as long as I live, when it comes to weight loss it can become an unrealistic panacea.

Unfortunately, many people consistently underestimate how much exercise is required to burn off extra calories. One study showed it took forty-five minutes of swimming to burn off the calories in one slice of pepperoni pizza. One slice? I don't think I've ever eaten less than six pieces in a sitting. I'd have to swim the Atlantic Ocean to burn off my pizza consumption. Another study showed that it takes two hours of cycling to burn off the calories of two doughnuts. Given my habitual consumption of Krispy Kreme doughnuts at the airport I'd clearly be better off skipping the plane flight altogether and just cycling home instead. If you don't believe me, just get on a treadmill at the gym and watch how slowly the calorie counter ticks over.

I've known a number of people who exercised every day and still struggled with their weight. On one occasion I had to talk a colleague out of committing to going to lunchtime, as well as morning and evening, aerobics classes to shift the stubborn pounds.

If you're not doing *any* exercise you should definitely work some into your routine. However if you are overweight and currently doing thirty minutes of exercise four or five times a week it's unlikely to be lack of exercise that's your issue.

The second part of the problem with exercise is that, just like we underestimate how much we need to do to shift calories, we overestimate how much we can eat after that exercise. Study after study has shown that when we exercise more, we eat more.

I don't need to read the studies. I know from personal experience it's true. In fact I now realise that on many occasions when I've exercised I've gone on to consume more calories than the exercise had burnt off, and then some. So in the past pulling on my training shoes has often had the effect of *making me fatter*. Counterintuitive but true – and something I was now determined to watch out for as the calendar crept ever closer to 10.11.10 and the Wedding Cake Island swim.

And it's not just the obviously indulgent things like pizza and ice cream that matter. One of the most surprising and useful things I'd learnt halfway through my journey to Wedding

Cake Island is that one of the side effects of regular exercise is that it can subtly turn your mindful margins into mindless margins. In the glow of having just finished a six-kilometre jog by the sea, having full-fat milk rather than skim seems no big deal. Same with having a small bit of butter on your toast just this once. But it is often precisely these minor things that add up to destroy your chances of success. Over time the small things, cumulatively, have a big effect. In some ways the key to succeeding in genuine sustained weight loss is to remain 'mindful not mindless', which is not a bad mantra to help keep you on track.

I know this is contrary to what they promise in all those exercise-equipment and weight-loss infomercials on TV but, irrespective of what the ads say, if you are going to lose weight you have to get your head around the need to allow yourself to get *really hungry* on a regular basis.

I realise neither of the above are the most effective messages to convince someone to buy a new fitness product or sign up to join the latest diet fad. It's far more effective to sell the dream and focus on the desired results without mentioning the uncomfortable effort involved. However, I'm not interested in conning anyone with an effective selling message. I'm interested in what *works*.

32

Who Put the Kiwi in the Lemon?

Much to Kate's amusement, six months after she had gone back to work she came home one evening to be greeted by me in the kitchen in a foul mood.

'All I've done is cook, clean and drive children around all day,' I snarled.

To her credit Kate resisted the temptation to point out that she had filled that role stoically for a decade and I had barely been doing it for half a year and was now squealing like a stuck pig. Nor did she point out the crashing hypocrisy of the 'I-want-to-leave-the-office-to-stay-at-home' writer complaining about staying at home.

Instead, she humorously took the piss and asked me to fix her a drink.

The truth of our situation was that, despite considerable effort, my progress in the kitchen was patchy. While my competence had undoubtedly improved, my attitude still left a lot to be desired. Also, Kate and I had a fundamentally different approach to certain tasks. Call it natural laziness, but I've always been a fan of labour-saving inventions. Kate, on the other hand, makes the conscious choice to take the most arduous option on certain occasions. Especially when it comes to food. Because for her cooking food from scratch is an act of love. Taking the easier option – even if it tastes as nice, is as cheap and is as healthy – isn't just lazy, it is in some way less loving. So if my publisher was coming for dinner, for example (as she was on this night), I wasn't allowed to buy a nice fresh organic tasty soup. No, I had to *make* a nice fresh organic tasty soup.

'This is so needlessly labour intensive!' I was heard to shout earlier in the afternoon as I whipped myself into a foul mood while 'sweating' the vegetables I had just spent an hour peeling and chopping.

That's not to say the kitchen was solely a source of irritation and drudgery. It also had thrown up a surprising number of joyous moments and rituals. One of these revolved around the plastic fruit containers I had bought at a dollar store at the start of the year. Fed up with the waste and expense of half-eaten fruit going off in our house I had invested the princely sum of three dollars on a plastic apple, plastic banana and plastic lemon. Now when we had a quarter of a piece of fruit left over, rather than leaving it to brown unappealingly in the fridge or cupboard we put it in one of these plastic containers and – hey presto – it stayed fresh for days. Particularly useful given I take Kate a cup of hot water and lemon every morning.

This system worked fine until the twins hit upon the side-splitting idea of putting the wrong fruit in the containers.

'Who put the bloody kiwi in the lemon?!' I yelled to explosions of laughter from the twins' bedroom the first time I groggily opened the yellow container to be greeted by a green piece of fruit.

From then on they started to put increasingly bizarre foodstuffs into the containers and I made sure to shout my annoyance loudly to maximise their amusement. It's not unusual in our household to wake up to cries of 'Who put the onion in the apple?!' It rather spoils the point of the original purchase, but it's fun all the same.

The kitchen also contains one of my most prized possessions. Earlier in the year Harry made a key holder in his woodwork class. It's in – you've guessed it – the shape of a large key. We stuck it on the kitchen wall and it is possibly the most used household device bar the fridge. The whole family uses it for everything from their house keys to the dog lead. And despite the fact that I must use it over a thousand times a month I *still* get a shiver of intense love for Harry every time I do. As an object it even bridges the gender divide as I can love it because it is practical and stops us from losing our keys while Kate can love it because, like the labour-intensive soup, it was made from scratch. Perfect.

The key holder is also an ever-present daily reminder for me of one of the most useful lessons I was relearning during this break. Yes, life is inherently full of compromise and littleness – but rather than fight it or try to deny that inevitability, our day-to-day existence can be transformed if we strive to deal with compromise and littleness with good humour.

And on that note I'm off to get the carrot out of the banana . . .

33

Are We There Yet?

One of the weird things I've found about taking a break from a conventional nine-to-five job is how it affects my attitude to holidays. Previously taking a holiday was an obvious break because I wasn't going to the office. Not going to the office anymore meant it was less clear. In some ways, holidays became a little bit more like work. I didn't really need a break to get away from it all – I had arranged my life so I was loving 'it all'. But hey, school holidays are school holidays and having four fractious kids clattering around the house all day for three weeks while I wrote in the garage wasn't fair to Kate or the kids. So we organised to go to a friend's holiday house eight hundred kilometres up the coast. When I was earning a salary we would have flown on one of the budget airlines but because finances were tighter, and because I wanted to replicate the enforced family time I'd so enjoyed in England during the snow storm, we decided to drive.

Now one of the things I love about Australians is the shared delusion they have when it comes to estimating journey times. They all deny they do it but, trust me, it's a national religion.

'Going to Byron? I'd leave nine hours to get there,' a friend at the beach told me.

Yeah right. There was no way on earth it would take as little as nine hours.

Another was more conservative. 'If you're taking it steady I'd leave ten hours, Nigel,' she said.

Ten hours?! For eight hundred kilometres? With the best will in the world that's absurd. But I'd long since grown used to, and indeed begun to enjoy, receiving ridiculous estimates. Over the ten years we'd lived in Australia I had *never* been given an accurate driving time. Without fail they're always pathologically underestimated. Driving to the ski fields? Five hours. Blue Mountains? An hour and a quarter. Jervis Bay? Three hours. All total bollocks.

It's as if at school Australians were taught to judge a journey by the *fastest* time it had ever been done. So, if your Uncle Jimmy drove to Byron in a Ferrari in the middle of the night in 1981, breaking the speed limit the whole way and not stopping once, and he did it in nine hours fifty-nine minutes, that translated into a general rule applicable to everyone – even a family of six in a Toyota Tarago – that 'It takes nine hours to drive to Byron'.

I've learnt to be particularly careful when an Australian uses the word 'about' when estimating a driving time. Just the addition of that one little word gives them licence to magnify the absurdity fourfold. If their definitive estimates tend to be on average twenty per cent shorter than the reality, the inclusion of 'about' before their estimate takes things to a whole new level. So the same person can be capable of saying both 'It takes nine hours to drive to Byron' and 'It takes *about* seven hours to drive to Byron' and actually believe they are giving the same time in each case. Once you've learnt the ropes it's actually rather good fun translating.

I've asked a number of people to explain this national characteristic and it seems there are two possibilities. The first is that because Australia is such a vast country people want to believe things are slightly nearer than they actually are because it makes the journey appear less daunting and gives the impression things are more accessible. It also encourages people to take journeys they might otherwise avoid. I mean, driving from Sydney to Melbourne to see your mates is a bit of an ask. But if it's only a quick ten-hour jaunt down the road, then what the hell.

The other explanation is slightly less flattering. This one maintains that driving time is a highly evolved antipodean form of penis measurement. The shorter the time, the longer the dick. If you say you drove from Sydney to Melbourne in nine hours it means you've got a really big penis, whereas if you admit it actually took you fourteen hours you're as good as declaring to the world you've got a peanut in your pants.

Well, at the risk of revealing I'm seriously deficient in the trouser department, the truth of our journey to Byron was as follows. We got up at 3.30 am to avoid the worst of the traffic and drove at the speed limit the entire time. With two adults and four kids in the car we made a number of short stops – two for coffee, two for petrol, one for breakfast, one for lunch and one emergency sick stop to avoid the car being turned into what the twins sweetly call a 'vomit comet'. I like to think we drove hard the whole way – we certainly didn't dawdle. And – drum roll, please – it took us twelve hours. I suppose we could have refused to stop, gone to the loo in bottles and allowed the kids to be sick in the car, but I reckon anyone who claims driving to Byron from Sydney takes ten hours has been smoking crack.

Not that I'm complaining. I loved the journey every bit as much as our snowbound UK one at the start of the year. So much so that, at the risk of being called a masochist, one of the first things we did when we got back home was book a campervan to drive around New Zealand with my brother and his family. If that doesn't beat the 'being cooped up in a vehicle with your kids for hours on end is really fun' attitude out of me, nothing will.

And besides, I'm reliably informed by one of my Australian mates that it only takes 'about' five hours to drive from Auckland to the bottom of the South Island, so we should be fine . . .

34

The 40-Day Plan

Our holiday in Byron Bay was even more fun than the drive there. We were staying with a mate I'd been friends with since university. By sheer coincidence both of us moved from the UK to Australia at around the same time and our friendship had only strengthened over the years. We became godparents to each other's children and, luckily, our respective partners got on just as well as, if not better than, the two of us. It was lovely to spend a week together in a house near the beach full of fun and laughter. Perhaps it was even a little bit *too* lovely as the neighbours complained about the noise twice.

Byron Bay is a gorgeous place, but it does have a slight hippy-dippy edge to it. To my mind that only adds to its charm – with one exception: the women in bikinis.

Now I have nothing against bikinis. In fact, from an entirely unreconstructed heterosexual perspective I believe they are one of the better inventions of western civilisation.

But I also believe context is important with clothes.

It's one thing to prance around the beach in your little string two-piece, but quite another to do your *shopping* in it. I get that Byron is a seaside town and the shop is just across the road from the beach, but there is still something not quite right about walking around a shop carrying a wire basket while wearing a skimpy swimsuit. This has nothing to do with body fascism. It's poor form irrespective of whether your body is old and flabby or young and toned. It's just that at a certain point swimwear ceases to be swimwear and *becomes underwear*. Just as you wouldn't go to work and walk around the office in your bra and knickers, walking around a shop in your underwear is not cool either.

Thinking about this made me wonder exactly where the transition from swimwear to underwear takes place. It's easy to decide at the extremes. It's alright to wear a bikini in the sea and pretty bloody stupid to wear one at the airport – but is it possible to agree on the grey areas in between? What about the café on the beach? Or the car park? Is a hundred metres from the water too far? Two hundred metres? Are you allowed to go further if you are carrying an accessory like a surfboard or flippers? I came to the conclusion that physical distance wasn't actually the best criterion. Better to stick to the simple rule that if you're standing on sand then it's fine. It's the moment you walk away from the beach and step onto pavement, or any other surface other than sand, that you should seriously consider wrapping a sarong around your bikini or pulling a pair of shorts over your Speedos.

Although in my experience it's women who tend to err more often when it comes to confusing swimwear and underwear, in their defence I suspect the error is usually one of forgetfulness. They need something and are just nipping up to the shops to grab it without thinking about what they are wearing – a subconscious sin of omission not a planned crime. No such excuse is applicable to a few of the men who share my regular running path who insist on going on their daily runs in shorts with no top. In these cases it most definitely *is* a body issue because it is never the fat and flabby who commit this particular crime. No, it's always men with the most perfect torsos who do so.

It's rare for me to go for a run along the coast path near my home without passing at least one hard-nippled poseur with his top off. And it's not as if they've taken their top off after getting too hot because they're never carrying tops in their hands, so have clearly left the house without one. Moreover, I usually go for my run early in the morning before the sun has had a chance to warm up and running on the coast path with the sea breeze coming off the ocean can be positively chilly. I quite often wear two layers and a beanie. No, these guys are determinedly and soberly choosing to run in public with naked chests.

Despite Kate's taunts I don't think my feelings are prompted by jealousy. I readily acknowledge that I would love to have rippling muscles like theirs, but I'm sure if I ever did I'd be more subtle about showing it off. There are, after all, a number of entirely acceptable ways of showing off your buff physique without looking like a vain plonker.

I'd recommend to anyone in possession of a torso they desperately want to show off the technique employed by the group I call the 'shirt-bottom wipers'. These are the people who, when they work up a sweat during exercise, wipe their forehead not with the back of their wrist like the rest of us flabby-bellied mortals. No, these people without fail *use the bottom of their T-shirt*. It doesn't take long and appears totally natural and functional – but we all know what they are *really* doing. And I guess if you've gone to the considerable effort involved in getting and maintaining a flat tummy you're entitled to flash it while you wipe honest sweat off your head. Longer or more frequent exposure than that and you should probably consider following the advice contained in the wonderful Australian retort, 'Mate, you really need to take your hand off it.'

•

Irrespective of how hot it got there was no danger of me using the bottom of my T-shirt to wipe sweat off my brow any time soon. Our holiday might have been wonderful in many respects, but it had been a disaster for my weight-loss objectives. When we got home and I stood on the scales I was horrified to find I'd put on half a stone over the week. That's a shade over three kilos – seven pounds in the old money. I was starting to feel like Bridget Jones. I was now back to the weight I was at the start of the Wedding Cake Island challenge.

More distressing still was that looked at in the cold light of day there was no longer any chance I would be 10.11 on 10.11. I'd failed, pure and simple. So much for using the power of my numbers obsession.

A key part of trying to move from fat, forty and fired at the start of the decade to something approximating fit, fifty and fabulous at the end of it was to have my weight under control. At the rate I was going I had more chance of being fat, fifty and getting fatter.

Why was it proving so hard? I like to think I'm an averagely intelligent man. And Kate tells me I definitely have above-average determination. I've been through a lot of change in the last ten years and have become quite good at implementing meaningful permanent adjustments in other areas of my life. So why couldn't I succeed at the modest goal of losing a pound a week? It was mystifying. But I clearly wasn't alone. A lot of other people shared my problem, including the three friends doing the Wedding Cake Island challenge with me.

There are thousands of people out there who try diet after diet after diet without success. The internet, bookshops and magazines are overflowing with opinions on the topic in general and I don't claim to have any new insights. However, on a purely personal level, I came to the rather shocking realisation that *I was finding it harder to control my weight than it had been to give up drinking.* I can't talk for anyone else, but the dramatic solution to my drinking issues (i.e. stopping totally) made it *easier* not harder. I had spent over ten years trying to cut back my drinking and could never crack it satisfactorily. Moderating wasn't the answer for me – abstinence was. But I could hardly abstain from food. So in this area – unlike smoking or drinking – I had no choice. If I was to succeed I had to learn how to be moderate. And on the evidence to date, it clearly wasn't one of my natural strengths.

It's not just that I found the weight-loss process physically difficult; I found the never-ending tussle between what I knew I should do and what I wanted to do, and the constant failure, mentally draining. And all day, every day, I'd think about food. I'd then let myself down by eating something I shouldn't or eating when I wasn't hungry and spend the next twenty-four hours hating myself. Then I'd read some news report about someone else's remarkable weight-loss achievement and feel even worse.

The day I weighed myself after returning from our Byron holiday was the day the last of the Chilean miners was freed and I can remember watching the news report and thinking to myself, 'You shameful sad little weakling. These guys have been underground for seventy days and triumphed over horrifying adversity and you can't even lose a measly pound a week.' It's a weird feeling to hold yourself in such contempt. Yet that was how I was feeling on an almost daily basis.

But I didn't want to give up. I couldn't give up. I had to be able to do this one small thing. I clearly needed yet another strategy, though. There was no way I was going to make my 10.11.10 deadline, but I was still committed to my 10.11 *goal*. The timeline might have to change but the end destination would remain. How to get there?

While thinking about a new strategy I recalled a story my other granny (not Vi) used to tell me about her days working at the perfume counter in a department store in Canada.

'Nigel, when a particular perfume wasn't selling well what do you think we'd do?' she asked.

'Ummm . . . cut the price in half?' I replied.

'No!' she exclaimed triumphantly. 'I knew you'd say that. We used to *double* the price. Worked every time.'

I decided to amend the principle for my purposes. If I doubled my efforts I could still make the Wedding Cake Island deadline. Losing two pounds a week instead of one would get me to my target in time for the race. If doubling the perfume price seemed counterintuitive but worked, perhaps I'd find it *easier* to lose two pounds than one. Maybe moderation wasn't my thing – perhaps *extreme* was. Maybe I was better suited to more, not less, challenging goals. Could it be the case that my moderate approach to the issue was one of the reasons I kept on failing? I was clutching at straws by this stage, so I resolved to give it a go.

To help me meet this new, more extreme weekly weight-loss goal I decided to adapt a strategy I'd used once when I was utterly miserable at work. Back then I was clearly misaligned with my employer and couldn't see the situation changing in any meaningful way. However, a number of people depended upon me and I neither wanted to let them down nor do a bad job. I had accepted the job in good faith and felt it was my duty to follow through with it. I therefore set in place a 400-Day Plan which involved telling myself that nothing was so bad that I couldn't endure it for four hundred days. Less fortunate people had been conscripted to fight in wars or had had to cope with horrific natural disasters; all I had to survive was a job I didn't enjoy. I would simply banish all thoughts of quitting and focus on doing my best for four hundred days and worry about what to do next only when I'd reached Day 400.

To my delight this strategy worked. I wouldn't recommend it to anyone as a long-term strategy, but as a short-term tactic it got me through. Like a prisoner in a cell, every evening before I left my office I ticked off another day on the 400-Day Plan chart I had drawn up. A fortnight after Day 400 I resigned and handed over to someone far better suited to the job. It might not have been the happiest year of my life, but without a doubt the 400-Day Plan helped me, and the firm, get the best possible result out of the situation.

To help me successfully lose twice the weekly amount I therefore established the 40-Day Plan. If I could stick out four hundred days in a miserable job surely I could survive forty days eating a little less? If for a moment I left aside the recent evidence of my specific personal failure, the general theory wasn't outlandish. Forty days and forty nights is, after all, a pretty well-established endurance timeframe.

People who train for a marathon will tell you of the Monster Month in their preparation program where things get serious and they take it to another level with a number of longer runs. Well, this would be my Monster Month. Two pounds a week back to back for five weeks until I was 10.11. Just like with the 400-Day Plan, there would be no room for questions or doubt. I could review things on Day 40 and not a day earlier. Until then I was going to tick off the days, and pounds, one at a time. And at least this time I didn't have to struggle with a complex set of issues that were largely out of my control. I had one single area that was entirely within my control to focus on. In fact, ten pounds in forty days when said quickly sounds the most positively straightforward and undemanding of tasks. Well, that's what I decided to focus on anyway as I embarked on Day 1 of the 40-Day Plan . . .

35

Bourgbarre

As I was putting the 40-Day Plan numbers into my diary I was struck by the realisation that in less than ten days our elder son, Alex, would be getting on a plane.

With our approval, Alex had applied to go on an exchange to France over a year before. Where had the time gone? For months the trip had seemed so far away it didn't really merit thinking about. And yet here we were with less than a fortnight to go till his departure. It had crept up on us like the ground rush at the end of a parachute jump.

Alex was going to live with a French family for three months. Given the family wouldn't speak English and Alex didn't speak French it was sure to be, as the Americans like to say, 'an opportunity for personal growth'.

Alex is a mad keen rugby fan so we'd requested a location in the south of France for the rugby culture. We'd also expressed a preference for a city location so he could immerse himself in urban French life. After learning he was definitely going to France, Alex spent enormous amounts of time getting to know, and following, the French Top 14 rugby tournament. Maybe he would get a family in Biarritz? Or Perpignan? There were so many wonderful rugby-mad towns to choose from in the region.

It had therefore taken us a while to orientate ourselves when a couple of months before he was to leave we received a letter informing us he would be going to Bourgbarre. Excited, we immediately searched the map of France, but we just couldn't find Bourgbarre. Until, that is, we referred back to the letter which, in our haste to search the map, we hadn't read properly.

'Alex will be going to Bourgbarre, *near Rennes.*'

Hold on a second, isn't there a Rennes in Brittany? I thought. That's Brittany in the far *north* of France. Yep, sure was. And right next to it in the surrounding countryside was Bourgbarre, which we Googled and found was a bustling metropolis of no less than 1813 people. Well, at least he would be in a village.

No, hold on, wait a minute.

'Alex will be living with his host family just a few miles outside Bourgbarre on their working farm,' the letter continued.

Great. So not the south, no rugby and no town. If 'two out of three isn't bad', I suppose you could say 'nil out of three is sub-optimal'. Luckily, we've brought Alex up to be a positive thinker and, to his enormous credit, he immediately looked on the bright side.

'Hey, Dad,' said Alex, peering at Google Earth, 'I think I can see a bus stop about a mile and a half from the farm.' He pointed at an indistinguishably blurred blob on the computer. God love him.

One of the things Alex's impending trip to France really brought home to me was *the awful, inescapable conclusion that our family life was coming to an end before too long.* Or more accurately, as Churchill said, we were at 'the beginning of the end'. When Alex came back from France he would be sixteen! He was already taller than Kate and me and spent a lot of his weekends out in the city with his mates. He would miss this Christmas and we might never be all together as a complete family at yuletide again. Ever.

Clichéd as it might sound, I knew he'd leave Australia a boy and come back from France a man.

He would soon be learning to drive, fending for himself and, when he could afford it, moving out. It made me feel short of breath. And chest-crushingly, head-achingly sad. I went to boarding school at an early age and have always been determined that my family would stay together for as long as possible. For the previous ten hectic years there had been six of us crammed into a variety of houses and cars, sharing everything, good and bad. I couldn't bear the thought of the six soon becoming five . . . and then four (I'd already told Kate that the twins could only move out after I'd died). Earlier in the year our younger son Harry had been away on school camp for just four days and while he'd loved it, Kate and I both hated it. The house felt wrong without him.

Embarrassing though it is to admit – and I don't know whether this means I'm in serious need of therapy, or just a mincing cry-baby, or both – on a couple of occasions when I was in my study writing I would sit at my desk quietly weeping at the thought of them leaving.

Therapy or no therapy, I clearly wasn't ready.

I shared my fears with a local dad who surprised me with the strength of his response.

'You have to grab every moment you can, Nigel. Mine are all gone now. I cherish the memories but bitterly regret the opportunities I missed when they were at home.'

It powerfully reminded me of the maxim that, in parenting, 'the days are long but the years are short', and it made me incredibly glad I'd taken the opportunity to be *able* to grab those moments. Previously, work commitments would have meant that there were limited opportunities to do so. School pickup at 3 pm isn't the most career-compatible routine, but during my time off it had become one of my favourite times of day. Particularly Friday. On Friday the agreement was that I, and I alone, picked up the girls from school. I arranged things so I had nothing else on for the afternoon. I took the dog, left my mobile at home, and specifically planned to *waste time*. As much of it as possible. I didn't rush the girls at the school gate. If they wanted to mess around with their friends on the 'top grass' for forty minutes it was fine by me as I had nowhere else I needed to be. If they then asked to go to the park, fine. The corner store? Fine too. Back to the park? No problem. Some days it took us over three hours to get home – and we only live four hundred metres from their school. Those three hours could be considered a waste of time, but to me they're some of the most magical 'grabbing the moment' three hours ever.

There's a real catch-22 associated with the childrearing years, which neither I nor anyone else I know has managed to solve. It's precisely the life stage when you need to be earning the most money to look after your family's wellbeing, but conversely it's also precisely the life stage when you'd ideally be spending the most time with your children as opposed to spending nearly all your waking hours in an office making that money. Alex's impending trip hardened my resolve. Financially my career-break timing couldn't be more appalling but, sod it, the corporate hamster wheel could wait for now. After all, it would still be there, whirring grimly around, when the kids were older . . .

36

Phone Lottery

My new non-corporate life was by no means all lazy Friday afternoon school pickups and indulgent dads-and-lads trips. There were daily frustrations that would test the patience of a saint. And, as Kate will readily tell you, a saint I ain't.

I might not have been going to an office, but I *was* working. Hard. Doing public speeches inevitably involves a significant amount of travel. And writing a book demands a certain amount of time to concentrate undisturbed – neither of which are entirely compatible with having four children. However unhealthy and unbalanced the life of an obsessive career climber might be, there is a certain liberation in being able to focus on one thing. It also makes success so much easier.

It reminds me of those professional athletes who win gold medals for swimming fast or picking up very heavy objects or throwing things a long way. On one level it's a fabulous and laudable achievement. But on another I just can't help thinking that it's all they've had to focus on for four years. If your whole life has been organised so that you can spend eight hours a day practising your craft while your support team looks after everything else, then you *should* be able to throw a discus a long way or move pretty nippily in the pool. My sporting heroes tend to be from a different, more amateur era. They're people who'd spend a week working down mines and then turn out for the Welsh rugby team on a Saturday and beat the All Blacks. Or that Australian swimmer, Andrew 'Boy' Charlton, who'd do a day's work on his family farm and then swim in the local river to train. Inspirational stuff.

And in many ways that's how I'd come to view working mums during this time away from the whirl of nine-to-five (well, usually eight-to-six) work. In most cases they haven't got the luxury of a singular focus. Especially those who work part time. It gave me renewed appreciation for all Kate's labours both when she was at home full time and now that she was working part time. And don't get me started on single parents. I am in awe of how they manage to keep it all together. Unlike sporting heroes they never get medals. It's just a daily battle. For years. Our society tends not to be very good at rewarding or celebrating quiet, sustained achievement. I believe we'd all be better off if we could learn to celebrate the ordinary and spend less time eulogising the extraordinary. After all, the ordinary makes up ninety-five per cent of your life so you might as well be comfortable with it or else you're in for an awful lot of disappointment.

So the truth for me was that while I was able to have many more wonderful moments of family togetherness, there were also many times when I wanted to tear my hair out and I quietly envied those besuited people who headed off to the city each morning.

My mornings were particularly stressful. I'd be keen to start writing, but Kate and I had agreed I wouldn't begin until the kids were all at school and the house had been put back into some sort of shape in readiness for the afternoon onslaught. A bit like Friday pickup, this was fine when I had the time and right attitude, but harder when I was in a rush and preoccupied. Talk about the Power of Now – there was no better lesson about the importance of being fully present in the moment than getting Alex, Harry, Grace and Eve ready for school and out of the house while worrying about the speech I was giving that afternoon or the thousand words I had to write before lunch to meet my delivery deadline.

It was even harder when Kate had a morning meeting and left the house earlier than usual. And it always seemed to be on those days that a forgotten project was due, such as the day a tearful twin came to me at 8.45 am and said, 'Daddy, I forgot to tell you I need to go to school dressed as a bridge.'

'No worries, sweetheart,' I replied calmly, secretly thinking, 'WTF?!'

'And it has to be Le Pont de Normandie,' she added.

Not just any bridge then.

'Okay, let's have a think and work out a costume for you after swimming on Saturday,' I said.

'No, Daddy,' she wailed. 'It's today. The presentation is *today.*'

Call me an absentee parent, but I'd never actually dressed a ten-year-old girl as a bridge before. I'm sure there was a good educational reason for me having to do so on this particular morning, but more than fifteen minutes' notice would have been appreciated, not to mention some sort of visual clue as to what Le bloody Pont de Normandie looked like.

An argument then started as Grace tried to get her elder brother off the family computer to get me a picture of said bridge. At the same time I was cooking them breakfast and trying to make their packed lunches. As usual, neither of the girls had unpacked their school bags from the Friday before. Their lunch boxes therefore smelt revolting and needed to be washed up. Same with the wet swimming kit that had been helpfully stuffed back into the bag to fester over the weekend.

Disaster then struck – the phone rang. I say disaster not just because it meant I'd have to stop what I was doing and speak to someone. No, I say disaster because I knew we wouldn't be able to *find* the effing phone. Because, despite her many wonderful, loveable qualities, Kate has one of the most annoying habits in modern history – more annoying even than her policy on random address book entries. For reasons that beat me, she steadfastly refuses to put the telephone handset back onto the base station when she finishes a call. The phone just ends up wherever she happens to be at the time: the girls' bedroom, at the bottom of the garden, the back of the garage. And she doesn't always leave it in plain sight; it might be on top of the dryer or under Eve's pillow. On one memorable occasion she left it *in* the laundry basket. It truly is a case of the Marsh family phone lottery.

On the dressing-as-a-bridge day I went into my normal routine of shouting, 'Find the phone! Find the phone!' The arguments ceased as the kids scattered to all ends of the house trying to find the phone before it rang out.

A mate of mine maintains that deciding whether or not to have a family is a choice between being irritated or lonely. I'm not sure it's that simple, but I can see where he's coming from. Another friend is twice divorced and when I asked him why he thought neither marriage had gone the distance he said sadly, 'Nigel, I've never made it through the young-kids stage. I'm not proud of it but both times it just tore us apart.' Obviously not ideal, but I prefer his honesty to those saccharine accounts of never-ending bliss that some people peddle. The BBC radio presenter John Peel maintained that whenever celebrities told him of their perfect blissful marriage he could guarantee that either one of them was having an affair or they would be divorced within three years. In his job he met an awful lot of celebrities and apparently he was never proved wrong . . .

37

The Undertakers

I don't want to brag, but I have *never* been beaten in a rowing race.

Ever.

That's right – in over forty-seven years I'm yet to be in a regatta where a competing crew has rowed faster than me in a race. My boat has *always* crossed the finish line first. Even five-time Olympic gold champion Steve Redgrave was beaten a few times in his career.

Whenever I remind Kate about this fact she somehow always feels the need to interrupt and remind *me* that I've only ever *been* in two races – both on the same morning and both against novice crews. Who invited Captain Bringdown for Christ's sake? It's a proud record and I'm sticking with it.

However, as someone who believes context is important I probably should admit that it is a *slightly* misleading account of my rowing prowess because until this year I had never once stepped foot in a rowing boat and to this day I have only ever done so four times. The aforementioned triumph of two wins in one morning happened at a rowing regatta on Sydney Harbour. Every year Sydney Boys' High School organises a Back to the Sheds Day where, among other more professional events, complete novices are invited to have some fun and compete against each other in teams of eight. For many, including me, it would be the first time we'd rowed. It's the type of thing that I never felt able to commit to when I was on the hamster wheel, but this year I jumped at the chance. For the five weeks before the regatta I went to regular 6 am training sessions for beginners on Saturday mornings to get to know the boats and how to actually row in a team. Hideously early as that may sound for a weekend morning, it is hard to describe quite how magnificent it was to be on the water as dawn was breaking and the sun rose over the top of the famous Sydney Harbour Bridge. I found myself almost pitying the poor millionaires in their waterside mansions who were sleeping through it.

I soon discovered that rowing in a crew of eight is the ultimate team activity. Unlike in some other sports, you can't just concentrate on your own performance. You have to be in perfect sync with your crew members at all times. The boat can only go as fast as the slowest crew member. It really is one for all and all for one. If one of you catches a crab (as I did three times), you mess it up for everyone, not just for yourself. To start with, it really was quite challenging. Because we were an inexperienced crew the boat rocked wildly from side to side. This was not just disconcerting, it made it impossible on occasions to get the oar out of the water at the end of the stroke. Hold the oar wrong and you're in danger of causing yourself excruciating pain by crushing your fingers against the side of the boat. If you're in the wrong position as you pull your oar you're likely to bugger your back by the end of the five weeks.

Then there was all the new terminology to learn. I had so many questions. Which end was the stern? What side was the stroke? What did 'tap' mean? How precisely do I 'feather'? It was a whole new language. Half the time I was so busy apologising to the crew member in front of me for hitting her in the back with my oar that I'd miss the fact we were supposed to be doing 'ten quick rigger dips'.

But stone me, on those rare occasions when it all came together and the boat was flying across the water with all eight of us in perfect harmony it was a magical feeling. And one I wanted to chase again.

My (albeit brief) experience rowing has given me an abiding respect for the people who genuinely excel at it – not just the Olympic rowers, but those kids who choose to do it at school. Having seen this shed's First Eight row, I can say with confidence that those eight seventeen-year-olds put on a display of efficiency, communication and teamwork that would put many a boardroom to shame. Not to mention the sustained dedication and commitment they clearly had to have to get to the start line in such fabulous shape in the first place.

Thankfully, all three crews for my races were comfortably at the other end of the spectrum to the First Eight. For one thing, we were all in fancy dress as tradition dictated. For the Rainbow Warriors that meant flowery shower caps and brightly coloured T-shirts. The Dawn Raiders were all in yellow, while we – the Mighty Undertakers – were dressed from head to toe in black. Black socks, black shorts, black shirts, black ties, black glasses and black hats.

We chose to call ourselves the Mighty Undertakers despite our complete lack of experience because we came to the regatta with one, and only one, aim in mind – to bury the opposition. There were three pillars to our strategy: trash talk, luck and gamesmanship. The name took care of the first, the dear Lord had to look after the second and our coach was in charge of the third . . .

'If you want to win, start when the marshal says 'attention', not when he fires his gun,' he briefed us.

Worked a charm. And so, on 23 October 2010, the Mighty Undertakers' two famous victories were permanently etched into the history books. Not that you needed all that context. Sometimes, regardless of what Kate says, context can get in the way of a good story and the plain facts should be left to speak best for themselves. 'Undertakers – unbeaten in this or any other century' will do for me.

•

A bizarre side effect of the whole Mighty Undertakers experience was that it made me think about work. Or, more accurately, 'conventional work'. This was not just because the training and racing reminded me of the satisfaction you can get from a shared team effort towards a common goal, but because ninety-five per cent of the other rowers were in conventional work situations and our conversations over post-training breakfasts naturally strayed into that area.

While I was still working hard, I was clearly no longer *at work* in a traditional sense involving a job, company and office. (Though I love the small damp storeroom under our garage where I write, it does have an ever-so-slightly less 'professional' feel about it than my old fourteenth-floor office with harbour views.) I genuinely couldn't have been happier with my current career choice, but realised with horror that the enthusiasm with which I sometimes expressed that happiness could be misconstrued as criticism of those who chose a more conventional route.

Nothing could have been further from the truth.

I have enormous admiration for those who choose to pursue a job or career over the long term. To resolutely put your shoulder to the wheel for the majority of your life so you can provide for yourself and your loved ones, while also contributing to the greater good of society through your taxes, is an achievement that should be celebrated from the rooftops by governments and commentators alike. These people mightn't have recorded a pop song or scored a Test century, but in my opinion they deserve hero status alongside working mums. Especially if at the same time as they labour they retain a balanced existence and a cheery demeanour – as my fellow rowers all did.

So let me repeat: I am not anti-work and never have been. I don't believe happiness is about arranging your life so you can just sit back and do nothing. I think real contentment comes from being engaged in an activity you find meaningful. And for most of us that activity is going to be what we call work.

As I was musing on all this I came across a poem that struck a chord.

I hate the bestselling book *The Secret* with a passion because I think it dangerously overstates its 'power of attraction' case and can badly mislead vulnerable people searching for answers in their lives. If your father has a terminal illness, like mine, simply believing he will get better and imagining him recovered will not work – whatever it says in *The Secret*. And yet I do feel the power of attraction is real in some indefinable way. Focus on something intently enough and relevant things and people do tend to come into your life. At least they have in my experience. And this poem was most definitely a case in point. I hardly ever read poetry yet, while thrashing these issues around in my head, a poem suddenly landed in my lap that went straight to the heart of the issue.

It's not as if the poem is a commonly known or widely circulated one. The chances of me ever seeing it must have been a million to one. Its origins could hardly be more obscure. It comes from the small village of Petersfield in England. A few years back the Petersfield Writers' Circle self-published a slim volume of poetry written by locals. A friend of mine, Vikki, happened to have a copy in her kitchen and I picked it up and flicked through it while she was making me a coffee. The poem in question was written by a seventy-year-old gent called Geoffrey Eyre who I salute from afar. Please look beyond the religious reference in the title and last two stanzas. It's a message I believe is equally valid for believers and non-believers.

Work and Prayer

Do not be in haste to give up work
No paid labour demeans a person
And a person at work, any work,
Is deserving of respect.

Do not wish for idleness.
Early retirement is slow death.
Work is the only lasting pleasure
And by your work you will be known.

Only fools dream of easy riches.
Legacies bring no luck
And lotteries enrich no one
Even those with winning tickets.

Poverty and sloth make cosy bedfellows.
Work and prayer are your stern parents.
Sometimes it is not easy to choose
the path of work and prayer.

Time spent at work is never wasted.
Time spent at prayer is time well spent.
And whether you believe it or not
work can be, and often is, prayer.

38

Rich Fuckers

Although my attitude towards work hasn't changed during my third career break I find my attitude towards the rich has. In a surprising way. I used to be consumed by righteous anger and hypocritical envy with regards to the wealthy. As our family's financial circumstances grew less secure the longer I stayed away from the office, I suspected these feelings would get more intense. Instead, the reverse happened.

For a variety of reasons Kate and I know a sprinkling of super-rich people. When I reflected on how their circumstances made me feel while I was living in self-inflicted poverty again I was struck by a couple of things. First, none of them are happier than me – which is mildly surprising given I'm averagely morose. Second, and more importantly, I came to realise that *all* of us are on the same continuum. I can no longer live in some sort of holier-than-thou bubble where 'they' are so needlessly rich and I'm so righteously living modestly because that would be disingenuous in the extreme. It's all about perspective.

A couple of months ago I was driving Kate and a super-rich couple home after a lovely boozy dinner. As I'm teetotal I always get the driver duties. Everyone else might be pissed while I'm stone-cold sober, but I actually enjoy it. It's a bit like when you drive your children and their friends somewhere; they tend to forget you're there somehow and talk revealingly as if you don't exist. Drunk adults do the same. On this particular night the couple in the back were very loved up and being all flirty with each other. I could see in the mirror the husband leaning into his wife and then heard him drunkenly whisper a sentence I shall never forget: 'Don't worry, sweetheart – if it all went wrong, if we lost everything and were utterly financially ruined, we could always move to Bronte and live like Kate and Nigel.'

Fabulous.

The place I have spent all my life striving to afford, the place that represents the pinnacle of my dreams and achievements, rates as their *disaster fallback position*. But I'm strangely comfortable with that because, although I may be poor compared to them, I'm revoltingly well off compared to others. And people who are less well off than me are fortunate beyond the wildest dreams of others still. Wherever you sit on the ladder, there will always be *someone* who thinks you're a rich fucker. Casting aspersions on millionaires with boats no longer stacks up for me, especially when they've done well for themselves through their own labour.

When I shared this revelation with Kate she could barely contain her delight, responding, 'Thank God! Does that mean you'll finally get over yourself and go back to work?'

Although to date I have no regrets about any of my career breaks, I've always been very careful when asked by someone if they should leave their job and take a year off. My initial response has always been: 'Under no circumstances can I offer advice because I don't know you and have no idea what your situation is.' One of the reasons for my caution is that for some people taking time off work is the very worst thing they could do. For a start, most people can ill afford it. But not only can taking a break put you into crippling debt, it can also have a seriously negative impact on your future career prospects and earning potential. We've all got to live in the real world, with real responsibilities and real dependents.

Even if I've got to know someone a little better and it's become apparent they could cope financially with a break from work, I've *still* advised them to exercise extreme caution. People tend to exaggerate the bad things about their work and romanticise the wonderful life they could live if they didn't have to go to the office. Having taken three major breaks from the workplace I know the reality of being a stay-at-home dad and working from home, and it's not for everyone. I therefore describe the frequent loneliness, the uncertainty, the lack of structure, the lack of status and the never-ending domestic tasks that can no longer credibly be dodged because you're at work.

One of the major lessons I've learnt this year is the all-important issue of how your partner feels about the idea of you taking time off. This has been a huge error in my thought processes about previous breaks. It should be an essential factor in your decision-making process. Even if you have the financial wherewithal to take a break and you're realistic and comfortable about the downsides I've listed above, I *still* wouldn't recommend you do it if you haven't properly got to the bottom of what your partner feels. And I don't mean what he or she says in order to be supportive, but what they feel in their heart.

Assume for the moment I'm talking to a married man who is considering taking a career break and staying at home. Imagine that up until now he has been the breadwinner while his partner has taken on the bulk of the responsibility for bringing up the kids and running the home. I would take pains to warn him of the devastating effect such a move could have on his wife. She could be enormously uncomfortable with having her space at home invaded by a stay-at-home husband. Moreover, she could be intensely irritated by him breaking the assumed arrangement re labour demarcation. If up till now the unwritten agreement was that he would go out to work and earn the money, or they both go out to work but he earns at least half the family income, it's not unreasonable that his spouse mightn't appreciate him unilaterally reneging on the deal without properly consulting her. She could feel deeply uncertain and insecure about the future. While his decision might be invigorating and life-affirming for him, it could be deeply depressing and frustrating for her.

As well as all that – and there's no gentle way to put this – it's *entirely possible his partner won't be as attracted to him if he stops work*. I'm not talking here about women who just view their husbands as walking wallets and run for the hills when things go wrong. I'm talking about real, rounded, loving, intelligent people. If the person they fell in lust with twenty years before was a thrusting corporate warrior it can be a bit of an adjustment to feel the same when that person turns into a househusband. Vigorously pursuing a socially acceptable goal like success in a business career is attractive. Some people, however subconsciously, *need* to see their partners striding out of the door, masterfully carrying a briefcase, to find them appealing. And I'm not blaming them. Everyone is different. While I like to think couples grow in love rather than fall in love, and change is a good thing, not everyone else does. Nor should they. The bottom line is your partner might not want you at home.

That's not to say you should stay in a soul-destroying job for the next ten years just so you can get your leg over, but your partner's perspective does need to be thoroughly examined before you do anything drastic. If you've read the above and still want to take the leap, I truly believe it can be the best, most joyous decision you ever make – both for your soul and your relationship. But hey, I would say that, wouldn't I?

39

Katy Perry

While I am a huge advocate of stepping off the corporate treadmill I have to admit that as I near the end of my third such break I've come to realise there are some things that, though they should be 'relaxing fun', will always remain 'stressful work' for me.

On my top-ten list of those things, organising and then hosting children's parties would occupy position number one.

I was reminded of this phobia recently when my soon-to-be-eleven-year-old daughter Grace asked, 'Daddy, why do we have our birthday parties in December?'

It's a fair enough question given she and her twin sister were born in the middle of July. And one without a very good answer. I like to think it won't become a permanent habit, but it just so happens that for the twins' last three birthdays we haven't got round to holding their party until December.

What's six months among friends? I ask. At least we don't hold it in a different year – which is an achievement of sorts.

I could claim that one of the reasons for our tardiness is that Kate and I run a pretty busy household in which it's a high-wire juggling act just to keep all the kids fed, clothed and alive. It's no surprise that niceties like birthday parties get lost in the mix. I mean, half the time I forget to send my own mother a birthday card. But to be honest it's not just a function of having a busy schedule full of competing demands that leads us astray on the birthday front; it's that I subconsciously – and consciously, if I'm being *really* honest – put it off for as long as I can.

It's just so damn stressful to get kids' birthday parties right. There are so many decisions – and opinions. Should we go out? Should we have a sleepover? What about entertainment? Who should we invite? How many? If we aren't going to invite the whole class how do we deal with those we aren't inviting? And then what about the party bags? Oh Christ, spare me the party bags. What should go in them? How much would be showy? How little would be mean? Could we get away with not even having them? The list of dilemmas is endless, and the repercussions of making the wrong call always seem so dramatic. The mere suggestion that Fiona the Fairy might be a little bit above Daddy's budget causes a meltdown of epic proportions.

And this is all before we even get to the day itself. Given we have four kids, we have held a lot of children's parties over the last sixteen years. Every sort of party conceivable, in fact. Yet on each occasion we managed to get at least one thing badly wrong, resulting in either offended classmates, bored children, a financially crippled household or a physically crippled father. (You try being the entertainment for twenty schoolgirls and see how you go. Encouragingly, I'm told backs eventually mend themselves.)

The actual party itself is perhaps the most stressful thing of all. Watching twenty or so overexcited eight-year-olds run wild in your home can be like having your very own live performance of *Apocalypse Now*. Few things could be worse than the combined noise and domestic destruction involved. Get some sugar into them when the cake comes out and basically all bets are off. Oh the horror, the horror.

However, this past year Kate kindly found a way to make proceedings even more painful. My wife knows my weaknesses better than anyone and is well aware I'm extremely self-conscious and touchy about my rather large nose, which made it all the more inspired that she substituted 'pin the tail on the donkey' with 'pin the booger on Nigel' as the climactic event of the party. This involved sticking a huge picture of me on the kitchen wall and watching as the blindfolded kids took turns trying to stick a piece of Blu-Tack boogie on the end of my nose. Her regular cries of 'Come on, kids, it's easy with such a huge target!' was a particularly fine touch.

At these events any attempts at imposing some modicum of control are futile. You truly don't know the meaning of the term 'ineffectual' unless you've suggested, 'Let's all calm down a bit and watch a Disney video.' Yeah, right. For my next party trick I'm going to bring about world peace.

Leaving aside the mayhem itself, on a deeper level it can be rather disconcerting to observe kids' behaviour en masse. Last time we had twenty ten-year-olds over I swear half of them were six and the other half sixteen. Physically and intellectually they develop at such wildly different speeds. One group might be off playing sweetly with dolls while another group is practising the latest pornographic Katy Perry dance moves. Thanks, Katy – having a bunch of ten-year-old girls doing pelvic thrusts in my kitchen really made our Christmas last year.

And apparently it just gets harder as they get older. Mates regularly regale me with appalling stories of bouncers, gate-crashers, fights, pashing, condoms found in spare bedrooms and vomiting teenagers at their parties. And those are the parties that went relatively well and didn't involve having to call the police.

As you'll probably have gathered, I find it all slightly over-whelming – hence the regular December parties for a July birthday. There is, however, one surprising upside. As a result of this harrowing reflection I felt slightly better about sending Alex on his exchange to France. After all, if we delayed his return by a week he could have his sixteenth birthday party in Brittany, not Bronte. Just a thought . . .

I couldn't help but miss Alex the evening I set the alarm for 2.30 am. England were playing South Africa at Twickenham. Since we had moved to Australia it had been a tradition that whenever England played a rugby game I got up in the middle of the night with my two sons, put on an England rugby shirt and watched the game live. As I huddled under a blanket on the couch with Harry waiting for the match to start, Alex's absence really hit home. For the last ten years he had been with us for every game.

I hadn't spoken to Alex in over seven weeks as we'd been advised not to make telephone contact. Apparently it negatively affects an exchange student's ability to fully commit to their new life, family and language. It had been hard, but I had followed orders and resisted the urge to call no matter how much I wanted to, relying instead on a fortnightly email update. Wonderful though it was to read his news it wasn't the same as actually speaking with him.

As the national anthems started my focus shifted to the game at hand. England were typically awful. At halftime it was 6–6 and all the signs were that the Boks would run away with the game in the second half. I reached for the phone to call my brother Jonathon in England for our regular transcontinental halftime match analysis, but before I could dial his number the phone rang.

'Hi Dad, it's Alex.'

'Alex!' I was overjoyed to hear his voice.

'Yeah. I knew you'd be watching. Aren't England rubbish?'

'Pretty bad. Foden's playing well though, isn't he?' I said.

We then proceeded to have the most wonderful conversation. It was as if he was sitting next to me, not halfway around the world on a farm in France. We spoke about the game, his host family, the appalling French winter, his school in Rennes.

I woke Kate up so she could have a chat. He even managed to make her laugh through her tears by telling her a hilarious story about how at school he was learning Spanish *in French*. Given he could speak neither language his progress was patchy to say the least.

To my horror, after five minutes Kate hung up without giving the phone back to me.

'He wanted to go as the second half was about to start,' she explained.

His Spanish might be a disaster, but clearly he wasn't having any trouble coping without us.

40

Count Ketchup

Though I now have a large family I *come* from a small one. Mum was an only child and, while Dad had two sisters, one of them passed away very young and the other emigrated to Canada when I was little. My grandparents lived far away. So when I was growing up our family generally consisted solely of Mum, Dad, my brother Jonathon and me.

Although every now and then I find myself wondering what it must have been like to grow up in one of those busy households with busloads of brothers and sisters and hundreds of uncles and aunts and cousins, I'm not complaining. My brother and I had a fun, loving childhood. However, with Dad incapacitated and both sets of grandparents long gone it really is only three of us left. So what did I go and do? Yep, I moved to the other side of the world. Brilliant. To rectify this geographical blunder I try to go back to England as often as possible, but with money tight it's not that easy. Flying a family of six to England from Australia is something I was happy to do when I was bringing in a decent salary, but it isn't really a trip you can afford to do on a writer's wage. Which is why I was totally thrilled when Jonathon and his family decided to spend Christmas and New Year with us in the southern hemisphere.

The idea was that both families would fly to New Zealand, meet in Auckland, pick up two campervans and then spend two weeks touring around the North Island. Unfortunately Alex would miss out because he'd still be in France, but five people squashed into a campervan would probably be more than enough, so maybe he was dodging a bullet.

We had the most wonderful holiday, packed full of marvellous times. Jonathon, or the Friendly Stranger as we call him, has a tendency to strike up conversations with complete strangers. Whether we were standing in the queue to hire a bike or buying milk in a shop, he would simply start talking to the person next to him as if he'd known them all his life. Bizarrely, unlike the woman I had accosted in the pub car park before Harry's school function, nine out of ten people responded positively, so not only did cousins, in-laws and spouses get on famously as we barrelled around in our ridiculously cramped campervans, we also seemed to share our holiday with half the population of the North Island as well.

We did all the usual outdoorsy stuff you're supposed to do in New Zealand – jet boating, whitewater rafting, hiking. At the tender age of eleven, Grace even did one of the big bungee jumps with her thirteen-year-old cousin Jack to claim the overall extreme-sports bragging rights. Our time together was very special irrespective of the astonishing New Zealand rain and the occasional bouts of car sickness brought on by the real (as opposed to macho-shortened) distances involved in getting to our varied destinations.

Not that the trip passed without incident. In particular I'll never forget Christmas Day. And not just because I've been left with a permanent physical reminder. There's a mental scar as well. Christmas was always going to be memorable as both sets of parents had agreed in advance that we weren't going to do presents. Or, more accurately, we were going to play the Present Game instead.

For several years I'd felt uneasy about our Christmas Day routine. However hard we tried it always seemed to end in an orgy of consumerism with the kids receiving far more gifts than they knew what to do with. Quite apart from the questionable message this was sending to our kids, it also struck me as just plain wrong. I remember my father telling me how for a number of years during his childhood he received a piece of fruit as his Christmas present. On another occasion he was given a *window-shopping* trip. When I recounted this story to my own kids I had to explain to them what window shopping was. It was clearly time to reset the bar when it came to Christmas Day for the kids. Hence the Present Game.

The rules of the Present Game were simple – each person brought one present that had to be either homemade, regifted or cost less than ten dollars. All the presents had to be wrapped in newspaper – no proper gift-wrapping paper was allowed. On the day itself, all the presents would be put in a pile on a table and lots would be drawn for the order in which people chose their present. But there was a twist. After the first person had chosen and opened their present, every other person had the option of swapping the unopened present they'd chosen for one of the opened ones. So quite apart from the shock the kids would experience on only getting one second-hand present, they would also have to contend with the very real possibility that if they actually unwrapped a present they were pleased with there was a distinct possibility it would be taken from them by one of their cousins or siblings by the end of the game.

We were well aware (half expecting even) it might turn out to be a disaster, but it was a risk we were prepared to take to avoid the annual present orgy.

As it turned out, the Present Game worked brilliantly and was hysterical fun. Each time a rubbish present was unwrapped everyone shrieked and hollered. The kids made a huge performance out of choosing whether to take someone else's present or unwrap the one they'd chosen. Kate had struck gold by buying a plastic ketchup-bottle top in the shape of a vampire's head. When you put it on a bottle the sauce came out of his fangs and looked like blood. Count Ketchup became the prize everyone wanted and bartered for. Presents, promises and a few tears from the younger ones were all expended in pursuit of this, the ultimate present. It wasn't quite as austere as giving them a piece of fruit each, but the total expenditure for both families can't have been more than fifty dollars – and without a doubt it was one of the best Christmas-present sessions the family had ever had. No one complained they didn't have enough presents or they weren't good enough and after the game finished everyone happily piled off to the campsite water park. The kids *still* talk about the game six months later and we intend a repeat performance next Christmas.

After the game Kate called her mum and dad to wish them a happy Christmas and ended up having a lovely conversation about their recent visit to Alex in France.

'You should be so proud of him. It can't have been easy but he's really thrown himself into things. His French has improved out of sight. His host father took me aside before we left and got quite teary, even calling Alex his second son.'

I was blissfully happy and had no desire to do anything other than chill out. The kids messed around on waterslides while I sat on the sidelines, nursing a coffee and reading my book. I didn't want to get all active and wet before Christmas lunch – I was just fine how I was, thank you very much. Until Eve asked if I'd join her for a ride on the waterslide.

'Please, Daddy, just one?'

'No thanks, sweetheart, perhaps tomorrow,' I said, knowing we were moving on to a different campsite the next day and would therefore not have the chance to go on the slides again.

'Oh, go on, you old grouch – it's Christmas,' said Kate.

'Yes, *please*, Daddy.'

I could see where this was going so, despite my irritation at a perfect moment spoilt, I gave in to the spirit of Christmas, put down my book, took Eve's hand and walked up the stairs to the top of the big yellow winding slide.

'You go first,' I said.

'Oh no, Daddy – we'll go together,' Eve replied.

'But it says here on the sign *never* to go down more than one at a time,' I said.

'Don't be silly, Daddy. Grace, Harry, Mum and I have been going down as a foursome all morning. It's fun.'

'I'm not sure, sweetheart. It seems a bit dangerous to me.'

'Mum! Daddy's being Captain Bringdown again,' Eve shouted to Kate and Grace, who were waving from the pool below. Everyone else within a four-hundred-metre radius would no doubt have heard this update on my parental inadequacies given the impressive volume of Eve's voice.

Lovely. Nothing like being publicly denounced as a party pooper on Christmas Day.

'Okay then, how do we do this?' I asked, thinking there'd be no harm in doing it just once.

'Easy, Dad,' said Eve. 'I just sit on your lap and we whizz down.'

'But won't I land on you at the end?' I asked.

'That's half the fun, Daaaaad,' she said in a tone that implied I wasn't just being wimpy but utterly moronic as well.

'Alright then, hop on,' I said.

And off we went. It was fun. And I did land on her at the end. And it didn't in any way hurt her.

But it did break my toe.

Yelling with anger and pain, I hopped out of the pool to see that one of the toes on my right foot was bent at a right angle.

I'm not sure if it was concern over a lawsuit or the severity of the break, but when I showed it to one of the pool attendants he offered to drive me to the hospital immediately. So despite all my dreams of dozing by the pool followed by a long lazy lunch, I actually spent five hours of Christmas Day in the casualty ward of Lake Taupo Hospital.

Thankfully, the staff at the hospital were fabulous. After an understandable delay (it was Christmas Day, after all), they explained there was bugger-all you could do with a broken toe apart from bend it back into shape and strap it to the toe next to it. Before they did so, however, they took me to the main ward and asked me to sit on a bed until an X-ray machine became available. The bed had a retractable wall of curtains on either side but was open to the main thoroughfare that linked all the beds. I sat down and picked up an out-of-date trashy celebrity magazine to fill the time just as a huge tattooed Maori bloke in dirty shorts and a singlet walked past and boomed, 'This is fucked, isn't it, bro?'

'Er, well it's not exactly how I'd planned to be spending my Christmas, no,' I replied, wincing at his language given the number of kids and women within earshot awaiting treatment.

'I don't fucking need this bullshit. I shouldn't even be here!' he said angrily.

After a quick scan of him I couldn't see any obvious signs of injuries. Though I didn't really want to encourage conversation with someone who looked so intimidating, I was about to ask why he was at the hospital when a nurse appeared in the corridor with a young girl.

'We've cleaned the cut and given her a thorough examination – she's only going to need two or three butterfly stitches and then she'll be right to go back home,' the nurse said kindly to both the girl and the bloke who I now assumed was her father.

Looking at the girl, I thought she couldn't have been much more than six years old – seven at the most. She had a bruise and a freshly cleaned gash on her forehead. And though any of my kids would have relished being the centre of attention in her situation, this little girl seemed cowed as she stared at the floor by her feet.

'This is bullshit! I've got gaffer tape in the van. I could have sorted this myself. Fucking women! I told my wife I didn't need to take her to the hospital.' The man grabbed the little girl's arm and yanked her to his side.

The nurse, with incredible calm, knelt down and said to the girl, 'We're just going to put some butterfly plasters on your head, sweetheart. Your daddy will be here when you return.' She then took the girl's arm back from her father and walked her away out of my sight.

The father's veins were bulging in his neck above his stained singlet by this time. He turned to me and said, 'I told you this was fucked, bro. Fucking women. Fucking nurses. I don't need this shit. Fucking Christmas. Fucking hospital.'

I'm very rarely lost for words, but I had absolutely no idea what to say. My mind, however, was racing. It seemed likely that this man was a child batterer and that under no circumstances should the young girl be put back into his care. But of course that's exactly what happened.

Ten minutes later I clearly heard the girl being handed over and the father effing and blinding about 'fucking nurses' and 'fucking doctors' as he left without so much as a thank you or a happy Christmas.

I'm told I will have a permanently crooked toe on my right foot, but that isn't what I will remember from that Christmas Day. Neither will it be the Present Game or Count Ketchup. However hard I try, I can't rid myself of the stories I've made up in my mind about that girl and her fate. It's entirely possible that I have an overactive imagination and everything was actually fine and innocent. I certainly hope so. Even if I'm right and there was a problem, I've been assured by numerous people that every hospital has procedures in place for following up suspicious cases involving domestic violence. Nonetheless, Christmas Day in New Zealand will forever be linked in my mind to that little girl.

41

Slow Down, You're Here

The second half of our New Zealand trip was every bit as enjoyable as the first, though quite different – and not just because I was hobbling around and couldn't join in all the physical activities with the others. For a start we did less driving around in our campervans as for a wonderful four days we stayed with my brother's delightful in-laws in Hawkes Bay before Jonathon and his family flew back to the UK. After that we swapped the campervan for a beachside cottage on Waiheke Island.

Up until then I'd thought I'd found my favourite place on the planet when I visited Lord Howe Island for my fortieth birthday. However, Waiheke Island gives Lord Howe a damn good run for its money. A small island just twenty kilometres off the Auckland coast, Waiheke is accessed by a short ferry ride. The first thing you see when you drive off the ferry onto the island is a road sign that says, simply: SLOW DOWN, YOU'RE HERE. I fell in love with the place immediately. I mean, how cool is that? *Slow down, you're here.* It's more than a suggestion about driving speeds – it's a *philosophy for life.* Really, in an increasingly stressed and busy world, slowing down is a radical act. We could all afford to slow down a bit, taking the time to appreciate what we've got and live in the moment – which is precisely what we intended to do while on this island, the natural beauty and serenity of which lent itself to such a purpose perfectly.

Waiheke is only nineteen kilometres long, and in places less than a kilometre wide, but because of its uneven shape it has over a hundred and thirty kilometres of coastline – forty kilometres of which are sandy. As a result, there are seemingly limitless beaches to choose from. My favourite was Palm Beach, which I found one morning after I got up early and, leaving the rest of the family asleep, set out in the car for an exploratory drive with a takeaway coffee and a map of the region. Less than ten minutes into my drive – bam! – there was Palm Beach.

I loved Palm Beach not only for its crystal-clear waters, huge expanse of sand, beautiful bay and lack of crowds, but because at the western end of the main beach there was a completely secluded nudist beach that could only be reached by climbing over a line of jagged rocks that extended from the cliffs all the way into the sea. No man could have done a better design job than nature in screening one beach from another. If you wanted your conventional beach experience, you could turn right. If you fancied getting your kit off in total privacy, you turned left.

What's more, having parked the car and walked down to check out the beach on my first visit to Palm Beach, I was both surprised and delighted to see a Quaker meeting house set back slightly from the beach. Now, over many years of trial and error, I've settled on the extremely low-church Quakers as the preferred denomination for my infrequent formal worship. I'm happy for people to believe whatever they want, but personally I just can't rid myself of the feeling that if Jesus returned any time soon he'd find many of the more formal Christian churches entirely contradictory to his message.

It's hard to express just how unlikely finding a Quaker house at Palm Beach, Waiheke Island, was. Because although the Quakers are a lovely bunch, they are also *spectacularly* useless at selling themselves. They simply can't bring themselves to recruit. Their approach is: 'If you'd like to come along, great; if not, that's fine too because you've probably got other things to do and we understand. Let us know if you ever change your mind.' I've got one of their 'promotional pamphlets' at home, which says: 'New members are always welcome. We have a wide tolerance of other religions and respect for their truths. We do not put pressure on anyone to join our society.' And this is their *recruitment* literature. Somehow I don't think the Catholics or Mormons will be quaking in their boots.

The Quakers' soft-sell approach is one of the reasons I like them so much. There's no hard sell – just a loving, non-judgemental, no-strings welcome if you ever want to check them out. But while I love this laidback approach to recruitment, it does mean the Quakers are one of the smaller religious denominations going around. Current estimates put worldwide Quaker membership at three hundred and forty thousand. In New Zealand there are fewer than *six hundred* Quakers in the entire country. So to find a meeting house in New Zealand, let alone on Waiheke Island, is a bit like finding a Tibetan monastery on Easter Island. To my mind it just made an already perfect beach even better.

Having checked out both the beach and the Quaker house, I decided to bring the family back on the following Sunday. My plan was to construct the perfect morning to make up for spending half of Christmas Day in hospital. We'd get up late, Harry would bring Kate and me a coffee and the Sunday papers in bed in return for his pocket money (personally I feel child bribery gets bad press), I'd then drive the family to Palm Beach, go to 'church' (Quakers actually call it 'meeting', not 'church') and then reunite with the family for a group skinny-dip on the nudist part of the beach before lunch at one of the island's famed vineyards.

And that is indeed how we spent the first half of 9 January 2011. It was a glorious day of perfect weather. The family skinny-dip was particularly hilarious. The water was warm and we all spent a couple of hours laughing and frolicking around in the surf. If I had superpowers and could travel back in time I wouldn't change a thing.

42

George Clooney

Since we returned to Sydney from Waiheke I have met a couple of people who've taken a slightly perverse pleasure in informing me that Waiheke Island isn't as perfect as it used to be. Apparently, since it's been 'discovered' its character and unique laidback flavour are being steadily ruined. It used to be a haven for creative types and those in search of a sea change or a simpler life. Houses were cheap and everyone mucked in together, which gave the place a unified folksy island vibe.

Now, I'm told, the multi-millionaires have moved in with a vengeance and a lovely tumble-down beachside shack is no longer affordable to the average punter. Prices as high as twenty million dollars have been paid for existing properties and, what's worse, the developers have moved in. Apparently the islanders who want to protect the unspoilt beauty of their home are simply no match for them and their clients. There is an entirely sensible rule that no planning permission is given for any property to be built on the horizon line of the island. You can build your mansion on the side of a hill with a gorgeous view – just not on top of a hill, as that would ruin the island skyline for everyone else. A twenty-thousand-dollar fine is incurred by anyone who does so. Back in the day, that would have been a significant deterrent. Now, however, twenty grand doesn't even register for some of the people building houses there. So they go ahead and build McMansions on the tops of hills and just factor the fine into their building costs. Heck, think of it as a friendly donation to the council.

A wise man once said to me that, having travelled the world and lived for sixty years, he had come to the depressing conclusion that humans had two things in common – stupidity and greed. Stories like the ones I've been told about Waiheke's development tend to add credence to his claim. Apparently the 'true' islanders are now selling up and moving further afield to Great Barrier Island. I've made a mental note to check out Great Barrier on a future trip.

For me, part of the attraction of life on a small island is that it goes to the core of every human's deepest need – the need to belong. It can be difficult to see where you fit, or how you matter, if you live in a huge urban sprawl like Sydney or LA or London, whereas if you have to get a ferry home and only 7999 other people live on the same island it's pretty clear where you fit. You're all in it together. There's a natural sense of a shared destiny, community and interdependence. Whether you like it or not, you're bound by an inescapable mutuality.

Without the natural geographical belonging that a small island provides it's only natural that we devise ways of creating a sense of belonging. Personally, I join things. I'm a member of the local surf club. And the local swim club. And the squash club. Not to mention the Quaker house. And AA. I'm not sure if I feel this need for belonging more keenly because I come from a military family and we were always moving every few years, but it's true I want a sense of belonging to something. I want to be a part of something bigger than myself. Something local and tangible. Not something viral on the internet but something I can touch, see and walk to. Because local matters.

Physical location used to define our belonging, but this geographical logic is no longer a given. Technology now gives us the capacity to create connections with people who live thousands of miles away. This is wonderful in many ways, but there is an increasing danger that we are virtually connected with people and events in far-flung places while being disconnected with where we actually live. And it's just not healthy to ignore next door. In fact I think it's a recipe for disaster for western societies. Reversing this trend will need to involve a *conscious decision* to engage with your local community, as it no longer just happens naturally.

It is yet another reason why I love all the community events that Sydney does so well. I do the fun run not just for the race or the exercise, but because when I'm jogging along the road from the city centre to Bondi Beach with seventy-five thousand other Sydneysiders I can momentarily convince myself that we are all one big happy family. And I belong in it.

Despite all the clubs I belong to, there is one type of club I have never joined – a book club. Until recently, when a local friend decided to set up a book club for a dozen of his male friends and sent round an introductory email. I was pleased to be included, but slightly dubious as we were to meet in a pub; since I no longer drink, spending hours with other men getting plastered in the boozer is not high on my list of favourite activities. My worries, however, couldn't have been more misplaced. The first session was hilarious and thought-provoking. It brought out the best in everyone. All too often men can get stuck in a rut where the only opportunities for socialising are sport and drinking, and where the conversation can tend to be more at the Neanderthal end of the spectrum. On this occasion, though, there was a refreshing lack of posturing or dick-measuring – just thoughtful discussion and good-humoured banter. It was an entirely positive experience and it's become a treasured part of my routine.

Unfortunately, the same can't be said for the only *other* time I have ever been to a book club. On that occasion I wasn't a member of the club. I was the author. A reader had sent me a delightful email inviting me to her book club as they were going to be discussing my first book, *Fat, Forty and Fired*. She completely understood if I was too busy or wasn't interested, but she'd promised her friends she'd at least ask me.

As I said, I'd never been to a book club before but I thought: what the hell, why not? Apart from anything else I presumed they wouldn't have invited me if they'd hated the book so it had all the hallmarks of being a pleasant evening where people said nice things to me.

And so it proved. In fact, in my wildest dreams I couldn't have imagined the love fest I was treated to. It's not often that I get to enjoy the fabulous feeling of being attractive to women. I'd like to tell you I'm above all that and found it embarrassing and awkward, but the truth is I *loved* it.

The questions they went on to ask me were well informed and interesting, though mostly on the same theme. They seemed to have formed the opinion from the book that I really understood the female perspective and could genuinely empathise with their hopes, dreams and fears. Most of them had marked pages and taken notes and they referred to them frequently in our discussions. It must have been the wine but I could have sworn they were flirting with me. By halfway through the evening the air was positively crackling with sexual tension. So this is what it must feel like to be George Clooney, I thought.

As the evening wore on, however, the tone of the questions became slightly more difficult to ignore.

'Nigel, the bit I most loved was the passage where you describe the argument you had with your wife about dressing your twin daughters,' said the attractive thirty-year-old with the low-cut top, leaning across the table.

'Oh, really? Why that scene in particular?' I replied in as scholarly a tone as I could muster.

'Well, it was like you were inside me. The way you described how your wife felt.'

Fuck me, I thought, this was getting a bit out of hand.

'It was like you were inside my mind the way you described her side of the argument. It's so amazing for a man to write from a woman's perspective so accurately and compellingly. It's a real gift. I don't know any other male writer who does it so well. Could you tell us how you manage to do it?'

The whole group leant in a bit further. It was as if they were one multi-headed body – lips parted, cleavage projected, eyes wide – waiting for me to enlighten them.

I distinctly remember thinking I had two options. One was to play to the crowd and tell them how I had a natural God-given instinct for the female perspective. The other was to tell them the truth. In retrospect I feel like the man who turned down the Beatles, because I chose the latter option.

'Well, to be honest, when I first wrote that chapter I only included my own perspective. But when I showed it to my wife she insisted I include her side of the matter. She told me what it was and I wrote it down.'

And that was it.

Just as if someone had flicked a switch, the magic was gone. The group sat back as one. In an instant I had gone from that mythical longed-for creature – a man who truly understands women – to . . . a man. I'm not saying they were rude to me. They weren't; they continued to be delightful and charming. But the evening was obviously over. Glasses and plates were cleared away and the questions dried up. I was on my way home no more than fifteen minutes later.

43

Twelve Months, Twelve Lessons

One night I took our long-suffering dog for a walk and called my father. He still hadn't spoken since the God-bless-you call and I was emotionally prepared to be met with another wall of silence.

Not quite prepared enough, as it turned out.

Not because he spoke. He didn't. It was what he *did*, not said, that sent me into a spiral of heartbreak and guilt.

The 'conversation' followed its normal pattern, with me saying something, mentally counting slowly to seven, then saying something else. After what seemed like half an hour, but in reality can't have been more than five minutes, I wound up the conversation.

'Well, Dad, I'd better let you go.'

1 . . . 2 . . . 3 . . . 4 . . . 5 . . . 6 . . . 7 . . .

'Love you lots, mate.'

1 . . . 2 . . . 3 . . . 4 . . . 5 . . . 6 . . . 7 . . .

'I'll call again at the weekend.'

1 . . . 2 . . . 3 . . . 4 . . . 5 . . . 6 . . . 7 . . .

'Bye, Dad.'

This time I didn't wait for seven seconds but instead said, 'Nurse?'

Dad's carers listen in to my calls and it was my way of letting them know they could take the phone off Dad and then I would talk to them. The routine is for us to have a chat after Dad and I are finished. They're lovely people – angels, really – and I always make a point of thanking them for looking after Dad. Besides, it was soothing to talk to someone after five minutes of getting no response from Dad.

'Thanks so much for looking after my father,' I said.

'It's our pleasure, Nigel. He's a wonderful man. I really shouldn't say this, but he's a favourite here with the staff. Never causes any trouble and we have lovely chats – don't we, John?' She raised her voice at this question. I could imagine her sitting there patting Dad's hand as she spoke.

'How's he doing?' I asked rather redundantly as we both knew the answer. The shameful truth was that I had started to call less frequently because I couldn't help but question if it made any difference. Before she replied, I was suddenly hit with a moment of perfect clarity. *Who am I kidding? Dad obviously doesn't know who is speaking. Calling him is pointless.* I pride myself on being a clear thinker and not falling for sentimental tosh, yet I'd been harbouring this pathetic belief that when I called I made a connection, however small, and provided Dad with a glimmer of happiness. I just had to toughen the fuck up and see the situation for what it was. It wasn't my father on the end of the phone anymore. There was no one there. Dad was just a body without a personality or soul.

'He's doing so-so, Nigel,' the nurse replied. 'He has his good days and not-so-good days. But you should know he loves your calls. He made a huge effort and kissed the handset before I took it off him just then.'

I don't know how to properly describe what I did next, but let's just say 'drowned in a sea of self-loathing' would be more accurate than 'walked the dog home'.

This latest conversation with my father caused me to seriously reflect. My visit to his nursing home had been pivotal in my decision to take this career break. Now, as the twelve-month anniversary of me leaving the office for the third time was approaching, I wondered what lessons I'd learnt from the experience this time around. Apart from the obvious fact that Louise, Steven, Thomas and I were equally useless at losing weight, I came up with a dozen.

The first was that at my age a year isn't actually very long. It takes a surprising amount of time to get the corporate life and attitude totally out of your system. Hard though it might be for executives who've never taken a career break to believe, that two-month long-service leave you're looking forward to just might not be long enough to effect any significant change in your life. Sure, you'll have a fabulous holiday, but you might find that's *all* it is and nothing has really changed by the time you've returned to work.

Once I got the corporate world out of my system, far from being bored or at a loss for things to do, the time flew by and I'd rarely been busier – or happier. As the weeks passed I found my gratitude level was gradually reset. Logically, I knew I was enormously fortunate, but I also came to *feel* it – deeply. I began to count my blessings as a default setting. I mean, how lucky was I to be born and live in a free prosperous country? And to have received an education and have my health? And a family? It's ridiculously good fortune. Especially if you think about the circumstances of so many others. Why staying at home rather than going to an office would inspire these reflections I have no idea, but it did.

I read somewhere that true happiness is when what you think, what you say and what you do are in alignment. On the basis of the past year I think that's true. Not having to pretend is a huge blessing. I never want to be rude to anyone, but I did treasure the fact that I no longer had to pretend I believed things I didn't or pretend to be someone I'm not.

A huge factor in the enjoyment of my time off had been the time I spent with the kids. Challenging though they may occasionally be, they are a never-ending source of joy as well. One of the cruellest ironies in many men's working lives is that by the time they finally have the opportunity and financial wherewithal to spend time with their kids *they've already left home.*

Alex had by now returned from France. His grandparents had been right; his French had improved out of sight. Not only did he now have his Facebook settings in French, but the first time we visited the beach he spent a good five minutes speaking it to the pretty backpacking waitress who brought us our coffee. But it wasn't just his language skills that had changed – he was taller, more mature, more independent. It was clear we wouldn't have him at home for long.

I will therefore be forever grateful that I was lucky enough to have three years with the kids while they were still at home.

Lesson number two was that kids know when you're bored or irritated by them – and they equally know when you love spending time with them. A few years ago a friend I admire enormously told me the secret to successful parenting was learning to *enjoy* your kids. They are words I have tried to live by. A perfect example of the beneficial effect this attitude can have came only last week when my eldest got his L plates. A quirk of Australian law is that you can't progress to your P plates until you've done one hundred and twenty hours with a parent (or other licensed driver) in the passenger seat. That's a lot of time spent in white-knuckled terror as you're driven around busy city streets by an inexperienced teenager. Between Kate and I, we will have to spend a total of four hundred and eighty hours in such a state before they can all go off on their own. And I'm actually immensely grateful for such a perfect excuse to spend time with them one on one. As they get older and more independent it may be the only significant time I'll have with them.

My third lesson was about change. Personal change. As I look back I've learnt that if you intend to make meaningful permanent changes in your life you need to be careful about where your motivation is coming from. If you are getting it externally, you are in for a fall. Trying to change so you get the attention, affirmation and approval of others simply doesn't work. For a start you probably won't get the attention you desire anyway as other people simply aren't as interested in us as we like to kid ourselves. But even if you do get the attention and praise you crave – *it won't last*.

In the first week after I gave up drinking I was a hero. People fell over themselves to tell me how impressive they found my determination and resolve. Three months later I was the boring bastard who drank orange juice. If I'd been giving up booze for others, I would have been sunk. The same goes for whatever area you are addressing in your life. Many years ago Jesse Owens said, 'The only victory that matters is the victory over yourself' and this statement is every bit as relevant today as it was then. Being internally motivated is essential if you're to succeed in the long term.

My fourth lesson was that long term is the time scale that matters. Any buffoon can effect short-term ephemeral change. It's making permanent changes that's the real game. And this takes time. It took me ten tears of trying and failing before I gave up drinking. Breaking old habits and establishing new ones is hard. The trick is not to view the failures and lapses as a waste of time, but rather as helpful building blocks on the way to finally succeeding. I constantly struggle with my weight. But each time I fail to lose as much as I want I still feel I'm getting nearer to succeeding and finally cracking it.

The fifth lesson I learnt was that when you do reach a goal you have to realise it's only one moment in time and without constant vigilance it's easy to slip back to your old ways again. Despite all of us failing the Wedding Cake Island challenge, I have recently reached my ideal weight. But how long will that last? Apart from an initial 'Woohoo!' on the morning the scales finally showed the right number I'm well aware there is no finish line.

Meaningful change is not only a long-term process but an ongoing one. I don't want to run one ten-kilometre race in under fifty minutes – I want to be fit and active into my old age. I don't want to cook a big family meal once a week and expect a round of applause – I want to learn how to fully contribute to the domestic daily chores so I can *effectively* relieve the unfair burden on Kate. I don't want to heroically reach my goal weight for a week and then blow out yet again a month later – I want to be slim on an ongoing basis. And perhaps most importantly, I don't want to have another year off and then unhappily go back to a job that I'm misaligned with – I want to learn how to live, love and provide for my family, and contribute to society, in a way that is true to my values.

Which brings me to my sixth lesson – I've finally given up on any notion of striving for perfection. George Orwell was right when he said: 'The essence of being human is that one does not seek perfection.' *Meaningful sustainable progress* is now my benchmark rather than instant perfection or one-off victories. I am quietly pleased with some of the progress I've made in core areas of my life over the last few years, but I'm under no illusions. I know how much work I have to do if my fifties are in any way to live up to my dreams and hopes.

Seventh, I've come to believe that by the time you reach fifty the real battle is rarely in discovering new answers – it's in *implementing the old ones you already know.* I'm not suggesting people magically become wise and have nothing more to learn on reaching fifty. But people do tend to develop the capacity to see through the false promise of there being a never-ending stream of new answers out there that will finally solve our problems. Whatever area of our lives we want to change, we are hardwired to be attracted to the latest fashionable quick fix – in our business lives as well as our personal lives. It's easier to read the latest business or diet book than actually fix your business and waistline. But the truth is your granny was probably right with all her clichés about the early bird getting the worm, hard work and persistence, etc. The latest business or diet book is just delaying you when you should be attending to the things that you already know you should be doing – like eating less and satisfying your customers. My repeated invention of ever more new weight-loss strategies just goes to prove that's definitely true for me – the 40-Day Plan, number coincidences and joint team resolutions were simply excuses to enable me to focus on anything but the one thing that works: eating less. So now I try to remind myself to spend more time working on actually achieving my goals than inventing new ways in which I *might* achieve them. More doing, less theorising.

My eighth lesson involves hard work. It'd be impossible for nearly anyone to become a concert pianist without putting in serious and sustained long-term effort and making a load of mistakes. So I don't know why I ever thought working out how to live a more balanced authentic life would be a simple, quick or linear process. Whatever path you choose, there is no alternative for ninety-nine per cent of us other than hard lifelong slog and course corrections. 'Life is struggle, content-ment is death,' as Gavin, a mate of mine at the surf club, said to me recently. Where we *have* got a choice is what we slog *at*. My quest, as I face fifty, isn't about avoiding hard work or difficult challenges – it's about redefining success on my terms and choosing to work hard chasing the things *I* value.

And this is lesson number nine. It's okay not to chase the things mainstream society values – or even the things you yourself valued twenty years ago. Just like you grow in love, you grow in labour. I spent twenty-five years chasing a traditional view of success. I've no complaints – as a young buck it was enormous fun climbing the greasy pole and getting pissed in the business lounge. But as a soon-to-be fifty-year-old I've realised I need a different, more wholehearted approach if I'm to be proud of my contribution during the second half of my life. I don't want to be a one-dimensional corporate hamster, but neither do I want to be a slothful couch potato. I want to contribute and be connected in a way I find purposeful and meaningful.

Authenticity as a word has been badly overused, mainly by the corporate sector. But nevertheless my tenth lesson is that finding a place in the world where you can be authentic is the greatest gift in this life and, indeed, my dearest wish for my children. I thank the Lord every day for my speaking work because, regardless of how good I am at it, I know it comes from a place of authenticity and is lovingly motivated. My intention, however small, is to entertain and help people.

As luck would have it I've had a modest amount of success in this regard. My speaking work has progressed beyond my wildest dreams. On top of the engagements I've always loved doing in Australia, I've started to get a steady stream of requests to talk at conferences around the world. I adore the travel, the new places and people I meet, the things I learn, the feedback when people find my message helpful – and as it turns out, it also enables me to humbly provide for my family financially.

Which brings me to my eleventh lesson. Real life is lived in the grey areas. Each time I've taken a break from the hamster wheel I've not only had a joyous time but improved my understanding of how to better attack my future. Working fourteen hours a day in a skyscraper isn't balanced, but neither is sitting alone in your spare bedroom meditating for weeks on end. I've long since given up any notion of chasing absolutes. Which went some way to lessening my surprise when I realised that my twelfth and final lesson was that I'd like to go back to work.

Traditional work.

Not immediately – I've still got some things I'd like to do outside the office first. But before I finally fall off my perch I'd like to have at least one other conventional role. Not to escape the domestic drudgery. Nor for a company I don't believe in. But at some stage in my fifties I'd like to put my labours to use in the service of others in a job that I could commit to heart and mind without having to pretend to believe anything or compromise on my values. Does such a job even exist? I realise my last three books are hardly the perfect CV for anyone searching for an aggressive, one-dimensional, focused alpha male. But I choose to believe being balanced, purposeful and authentic shouldn't exclude you from the business world. Indeed, you could make a powerful case that it's exactly what certain parts of the corporate world *need* at this moment in time. And besides, why limit your best self and thinking to the domestic sphere? Having had the utter privilege of being able to take yet another break from traditional employment, I am feeling refreshed and energised and eager to put my professional talents to use again.

Though this is not the conclusion I was expecting to come to when I started my year, if I'm ever able to get another job – which, as an unemployed fifty-year-old, is no small 'if' – at least I know one person who'll be ecstatically happy; and I susupect when I leave for the office it will be one of those rare occasions when she won't be giving an Armenian farewell either . . .

Nigel and Kate in New Zealand, 2011

Epilogue

Since finishing this book life has continued to delight and frustrate. The kids and Kate provide the delight; my inadequacies the frustration. Last Christmas is a good example of the former. This time, instead of visiting friends or family we did a house-swap with a couple in Hobart. Sitting at their dining room table looking at Kate, Alex, Harry, Grace and Eve screeching with laughter as the Present Game unfolded, I remember marvelling at how lucky I was and at how I couldn't imagine it would be possible to feel happier. I deliberately took a picture to use as my screen saver on my phone and computer to serve as a constant reminder of both the moment and the important things in life. Because, as they say, 'the main thing is to keep the main thing the main thing'.

As you could probably guess by now the frustrations are mainly caused by my manifold inadequacies. I remain a work in progress. Choosing a different path to a strictly conventional career continues to present its inevitable challenges – not least of which are compromises regarding your ego and finances – and dealing with those challenges is not always easy. One of the upsides of the 'alternative' path, however, is never knowing what's around the corner and the life-enriching surprises this brings.

One such surprise is that following on from my 'rowing success' I somehow found myself taking up basketball in my fifth decade. Of all the sports I could have imagined taking up basketball would be among the most unlikely. For a start I am hardly the right height for the game. Or, as my son Harry remarked recently while watching MTV, 'Daddy you look like a short Rod Stewart!' Given Rod is famously rumoured to be barely taller than a dwarf you can see the problem. My diminutive stature and the fact that I never played at school, or had ever stepped onto a court, means I am truly, breathtakingly, useless. Nevertheless, I am still a proud member of the Bronte Breakers – and loving it. Team sport surely has to be one of humanity's better inventions. To be able to enjoy its benefits at fifty and beyond is a wonderful privilege. Who knows? If I keep at it I may even get a basket by the time I turn sixty.

Most surprising, and joyful, of all is the fact that I landed a job with heart. Albeit a temporary part time job, but a job with heart all the same. It's a funny old world. Call it the law of attraction or just plain dumb luck, but out of the blue I met a wonderful couple called Andrew and Michelle Penfold. A few years ago in the middle of a highly successful legal and banking career, Andrew decided to change course and dedicate himself to helping address the moral obscenity that is the situation of indigenous people in Australia. His chosen route was via education. As a firm believer that good intentions are never enough, Andrew espouses a 'soft hearts, hard heads, capable hands' philosophy. In an area that is littered with well-meaning failure, his Australian Indigenous Education Foundation is a remarkable success. In a few short years he has raised the money to send 2000 indigenous kids to some of the best schools in Australia. Not satisfied, he's aiming to raise enough to send *7000*. Given the scheme is currently delivering a barely believable 90 per cent year 12 completion rate, it is truly nation-changing work. And I am now blessed to be able to play a small part.

I still get occasional flashes of anxiety that I'll wake up and realise it's all been a dream. But mainly I thank the Lord I've been so lucky. Just last week I found myself parking in the basement of an office block in the heart of the city. It was early in the morning and I was wearing a suit and tie. My briefcase was on the passenger seat beside me. I was going to a meeting in a company boardroom twenty-four levels above. Given all my agonising about the corporate world and my terror of being stuck on the hamster wheel, the situation had the clear potential to send me into a negative spiral of sadness where I again questioned the point of it all. Yet this particular morning I actually felt *joyful* because I was doing work I truly believed in and I felt like my efforts were making a valuable and appreciated contribution. Moreover, the project meant I was constantly being exposed to the best side of the corporate world. I was meeting and making meaningful connections with executives who wanted to use their success and power to give back and do *good*. It all made me slightly embarrassed about my previous cynicism. The reality is, two of the things I am most passionate about (AIEF and my public speaking work) are both opportunities afforded to me by the corporate world so who the hell did I think I was to be sniffy and judgemental about it?

Another nice surprise has been that Warner Brothers optioned the rights to make a TV programme of *Fat, Forty and Fired*. The chances of it actually being made into a hit series are so remote as to be laughable but hey, a boy can dream. In the very least it meant I spent a surreal week in LA. I realised what a different world it was on the first day when I witnessed someone being asked to help bring the shopping bags in from their partner's car only to be told 'I'd normally love to honey but today is bicep day at my gym and I don't want to pre-exhaust the muscle'.

Easy as it is to poke fun at the weirdness – after barely a day driving around in a sports car being treated like I was important by a bunch of Hollywood execs – I could see how circumstances could go to your head. Fortunately, the memory of the fate of the one-man play is still so fresh in my mind it's unlikely I'll get too far ahead of myself just yet.

I don't claim to have the answers on all the issues but I do know this: having been Fat, Forty and Fired, regardless what they say about the downsides of ageing it's a damn sight better being Fit, Fifty and Fired Up. Better for me. And better for my family. I might have no idea what the future holds for us all, but at least now I'm facing that future with excitement and positivity rather than anxiety and dread.

Nigel Marsh, Bronte, May 2012

Acknowledgements

To the readers of my previous books who have sent me messages of encouragement – thank you. It means the world to me.

To Tara Wynne at Curtis Brown and everyone at Allen & Unwin, specifically Louise Thurtell, Vanessa Pellatt, Ali Lavau, Darian Causby, Marie Slocombe, Louise Cornege and Allison Hiew – thank you for being marvellously patient, supportive and just plain lovely to work with.

Above all, to Kate – my undying gratitude for putting up with a husband who irritatingly keeps resigning from good jobs to 'find himself'.

www.nigelmarsh.com

About the Author

One of the co-founders of Earth Hour, Nigel March's speech on work–life balance remains Australia's most-watched TED speech with over a million and a half hits. Past CEO of a number of high profile advertising agencies, Nigel lives in Sydney with his wife and four kids and is the internationally bestselling author of *Fat, Forty and Fired* and *Overworked and Underlaid*.